the
Afterlife Codes

BOOKS BY SUSY SMITH

The Mediumship of Mrs. Leonard
The Enigma of Out-of-Body Travel
Prominent American Ghosts
Ghosts Around the House
Today's Witches
Confessions of a Psychic
ESP and Hypnosis
How to Develop Your ESP
ESP
World of the Strange
Widespread Psychic Wonders
Susy Smith's Supernatural World
Adventures in the Supernormal
ESP and You
She Spoke to the Dead
Voices of the Dead?
Strangers from Space
ESP for the Millions
A Supernatural Primer for the Millions
Haunted Houses for the Millions
Reincarnation for the Millions
Out-of-Body Experiences for the Millions
More ESP for the Millions
Life is Forever
The Book of James
The Power of the Mind
The Conversion of a Psychic
Ghost Writers in the Sky
Do We Live After Death?

the
Afterlife Codes

*Searching for
Evidence of the
Survival of the Soul*

Susy Smith

HAMPTON ROADS
PUBLISHING COMPANY, INC.

Cover design by Jane Hagaman
Cover art by PhotoDisc

For information write:

Hampton Roads Publishing Company, Inc.
1125 Stoney Ridge Road
Charlottesville, VA 22902

Or call: 804-296-2772
FAX: 804-296-5096
e-mail: hrpc@hrpub.com
Website: www.hrpub.com

If you are unable to order this book from your local
bookseller, you may order directly from the publisher.
Quantity discounts for organizations are available.
Call 1-800-766-8009, toll-free.

Library of Congress Catalog Card Number: 99-68263
ISBN 1-57174-191-7
10 9 8 7 6 5 4 3 2 1

Printed on acid-free paper in Canada

Dedication

For Mother,
for William James,
and for all those who
want survival to be true,
but are afraid to get their hopes up.

Contents

Introduction

Gary E. R. Schwartz, Ph.D.
and Linda G. S. Russek, Ph.D.

Throughout recorded history many people have hoped to be reunited with their loved ones after they die. Some have reported seeing or feeling the presence of the departed, but there has never been evidence sufficient to prove these occurrences to nonbelievers. Many who yearn for this to be true cannot even accept their own experiences because there is such a general attitude of disbelief.

Thousands of persuasive accounts have been collected from those who think they have had contact with loved ones after death. Others suffering near-death trauma have brought back stories of an unseen world, and recently the existence of special psychic abilities—extrasensory perception, or ESP—has been documented. Science, however, has not been able to substantiate any of this to its complete satisfaction.

Fortunately, the trend today seems to be toward scientific study in this area. Instead of challenging the belief in the Afterlife, modern science provides theory and research that justifies the search for survival of consciousness after death. A few academic books are being written by authorities in various disciplines who seem willing to discuss the possibility of the existence of a human soul, with implications as to that soul's possible future. Some people are even devising tests of various sorts to demonstrate a connection between Earth and the departed.

Among these is a system of codes offered by a pioneer of the twentieth century's evolving consciousness—Ethel Elizabeth Smith, known to the readers of her twenty-nine previous books as Susy Smith. *The Afterlife Codes* is a report of her careful forty-four-year investigation of spirit communication and her joyful, if possibly somewhat dubious, anticipation of shocking and amazing the world after her death with a coded message that reveals her continued existence. A former newspaper reporter, Susy provides accurate appraisal and evaluation of all her valuable experiences, and the information she has received about the Afterlife inspires and encourages further research. This entertaining book tells the story of her many exciting, and sometimes frightening experiences while attempting to mingle with the spirit world, and of her ultimate decision to leave codes (and make it possible for others to leave codes) that might operate between the planes of existence in an effort to give proof of survival after death.

We who write this introduction never expected to become involved in anything like the history and the legacy Susy wishes to leave. Both of us are scientists and clinicians working on the interface between physics, psychology and medicine. Gary was trained at Cornell and Harvard. He served on the faculty at Harvard before moving to Yale, where he was a professor of psychology and psychiatry, director of the Yale Psychophysiology Center and co-director of the Yale Behavioral Medicine Clinic. At present he is a professor of psychology, medicine, neurology, and psychiatry as well as co-director of the Human Energy Systems Laboratory at the University of Arizona.

Linda was trained at New York University, Columbia and the United States International University. For many years she was a research psychologist at the Harvard Student Health Service and was in private practice with her father, the late Dr. Henry I. Russek, an internationally known cardiologist. She is now co-director of the Human Energy Systems Laboratory and president of the Family Love and Health Foundation.

What has led us to speak out about Susy's research objective, and to try to test the survival of consciousness hypothesis? What has led us to go so far as to create The Susy Smith Project at the Human Energy Systems Laboratory? Our reasons come not only from modern science and our professional and personal histories, but also from our unexpected meeting with this remarkable eighty-eight-year-old woman.

As the late Carl Sagan, distinguished professor of astronomy at Cornell University, was fond of saying, "Extraordinary claims require extraordinary evidence." Research on the survival of consciousness hypothesis—clearly an extraordinary question—requires the design of extraordinary experiments. What is needed is a unique collaboration between scientists and laypeople that is deep and far reaching. Laboratory research on small samples of subjects would probably not be sufficient. Our thesis is that it will take research involving the shared visions and dreams of people from all walks of life to finally discover whether communication with our departed loved ones is possible. The Susy Smith Project was established on January 11, 1997, to continue Susy's long effort to study the possibility of the survival of consciousness after death. Its purpose is to bring careful and systematic research to bear on this fundamental question, and to assist others in leaving their codes in our computers.

Briefly, one way to test the survival of consciousness hypothesis is the way Susy has chosen—to determine whether a key phrase known only to a specific person can be communicated to the living after that person has died. This key phrase must decipher a code known only to the departed. Others have attempted this, but so far no one to our knowledge has been successful—with the possible exception of Houdini, about whom there is a good bit of little-known evidence that he actually did succeed. If, after Susy dies, the key phrase she has left in a fraud-proof computer with The Susy Smith Project should be broken by a living person, that person will receive $10,000, which Susy has left in her will for this purpose.

Herewith, then, is Susy's story of her personal research. She writes in her own colorful style for the reader who wants to be entertained, but she is nevertheless dealing with a serious pursuit of evidence, and hopes those with a scientific approach will appreciate the careful effort she has applied to her quest. Not naively has Susy become convinced over the years that she has been writing with her mother and a famous Harvard professor of the past century. She tells how she fought and argued and what accumulation of evidence eventually led to her happy acceptance.

So prepare yourself now for a good read that is also a philosophical experience and a heartwarming adventure.

ONE

Does E = MC^2 Scare You?

It is easier to talk about the possibility of life after death than it was when I was a girl, a long time ago—I've got eighty-eight years behind me now. Then it was considered impolite to discuss such things as religion, politics or sex because you might cause an argument or hurt someone's feelings. And, of course, at that time scientists looked on religion as a delusion of the masses. Now television goes everywhere, so we are faced with evangelical preaching along with shampoo, Coca-Cola and furniture polish. And as for sex and politics . . . we just finished the nineties, for heaven's sake!

In 1905, a brilliant scientist named Albert Einstein came along with his relativity thing: $E = MC^2$. It was unintelligible to most of us, but it means energy equals mass times the speed of light squared. Physicists have since begun to open their minds a crack, realizing that with that statement Einstein pierced matter itself and discovered that everything in the universe is composed of energy or force. As modern physicist Michael Talbot writes in *Mysticism and the New Physics*, "There is no ultimate physical substance to matter." Einstein is also reported to have said, "Anyone who studies physics long enough is inevitably led to metaphysics."

Metaphysics implies a thinking process, doesn't it? And thus we are led to the awareness that mind—consciousness—is the controlling factor of all this energy. Author-lecturer

Depak Chopra calls it "thinking non-stuff." Physicist David Bohm of Birkbeck College, London, says, "There's no sharp division between thought, emotion and matter . . . the entire ground of existence is enfolded in space."

Although this is difficult to comprehend at first, we can understand it when we think of the propeller of an airplane or the blades of an electric fan. When they are moving slowly, we can see them; when they are speeded up, we can't. So matter is energy moving so quickly—the speed of light squared—that we can only see it when it's slowed down. And the thinking property of matter, the animating force of life we call consciousness, is buzzing along so rapidly it is always invisible.

James, a spirit communicant I will tell you more about later, put it this way:

> Natural laws, which govern all of the universe, do not change. You can use them even if you do not know what they are or how they operate. A good example of this is the force called electricity. Now, the power of thought is a natural law little understood or accepted by you people at the present time. Yet thought power is the strongest force in the world, and the sooner you accept this truth and put it into practice, the sooner you will benefit from it.
>
> All matter can be controlled by thought, on Earth and everywhere else in the universe. If I had said this to you a century ago, you would have scoffed. But now the atom has been split and found to be composed largely of space and energy. Nothing but an infinitesimal amount of matter is discovered within the preponderance of space in each tiny atom; and this infinitesimal amount of matter is described by scientists as energy, force, or power controlled by consciousness.

About 1940, Stewart Edward White, a well known author of educational material for young people, began to receive what he believed was information through mediums from his deceased wife. She stressed particularly that "consciousness is the only reality and consciousness is in a state of evolution." Dr. Jonas Salk, many years later, referred to this as "meta-biological evolution—the evolution of consciousness."

That is what many of our scientists today are saying: that all matter, including the human body, is composed of energy or force controlled by consciousness—which lives in every-thing, forever. Modern researchers are becoming aware that even though we are encased in matter, you and I and we actu-ally exist as *consciousnesses* (or we can say "souls" or "spirits" if it won't distress the reader too much) and that our devel-opment as individuals of character and usefulness, of joy and love, is our most important function. "Love is the ultimate truth at the heart of civilization," says Chopra.

Rabbi Labil Wolk, interviewed in the *Providence Journal-Bulletin* in 1996, was characterized as "an explorer of Jewish mysticism." He stated: "Of course the notion of God in a mature sense lies in a more abstract area, an infinite source that underlies the reality of all existence not unlike what quantum physics is suggesting." Taking all this into consider-ation, wouldn't this overpowering consciousness, this energy that is eternally in everything—this invisible animating force of the entire universe and also the soul within us all—be God? An individual's consciousness or spirit or soul gradually becomes aware of its identity as an evolving human being as it develops from babyhood throughout life. At the death of the physical matter within which this awareness resides, the soul leaves, sailing forth into other dimensions of time and space. And continues to live forever as it grows in knowledge .of its unity with God.

Coming to this point from our start with Einstein, we have Paul Davies, a mathematician and physicist in Australia, saying in 1983, "Science offers a surer path to God than religion." Won't it be a blast to eventually learn who is right!

Of *course* there is life after death. There is always life and we are always part of it. The world is composed of nothing but energy, which thinks and is real and possesses its own identity. Some believe that stones, trees and sand on the beach—all things—think, in one way or another. It's easy to know this about ourselves, because we are thinkers of thoughts and we know we are thinking. It's almost impossible not to be thinking all the time, even when we long for sleep and can't silence the chatterbox in our heads.

Maybe sticks and stones know they are thinking, too, but we won't go into that here. Let's discuss instead how I came to be probing such deep subjects and why I think it is important to know that we continue to travel the road of spiritual development in an afterlife that awaits us all. While the physicists are doing this with their heads, I've been working on it experientially for many years. And still am—trying to prove it, that is.

TWO

AFTERLIFE CODES . . .
WHAT ARE THEY?

It occurs to me that readers might be wondering what codes have to do with the universal consciousness I've been talking about, and with the idea of life after death? I'll give you a hint. A code, or cipher, is secret writing meant to be understood only by those who have the key to it. In this instance it refers to a code that I have left in the computer of The Susy Smith Project at the University of Arizona. I plan after my death to send "secret messages" (key phrases) that break the code, to mediums, psychics or any other persons who are able to receive them. An award of $10,000 is in my will for the first one who receives the message and breaks the code.

The concept is that if you hear it from me when I'm no longer on Earth, it should suggest that I've survived somewhere after death. Anyone else who wishes to leave a code may also put it on our computer. (Directions are on The Susy Smith Project Afterlife Codes Website: *www.afterlifecodes.com*.) Discussion of the establishing of the project is found in my last chapter.

I think, and my spirit advisers agree, that it would be of great importance to the world to prove that there is a Hereafter. Knowing for certain that one was going to live indefinitely might encourage one to try to get off to a better start here. Accepting it on faith certainly has not been of any great value to the various religions, which have eternally fought over who is right in their beliefs. "Let's get some scientific evidence" has been my goal with all my research, and it will continue to be after I die.

The famous lawyer Clarence Darrow is reported to have said, "The truth is, no one believes in immortality." My communicant, James, who assures me he is William James, the Harvard psychologist and philosopher who died in 1910, wrote somewhat the same thing in *The Book of James*. He said:

> Many people do not ever think about the possibility of life after death. But most persons who think, think at one time or another about the subject—usually without achieving any answers that satisfy them. That is why they so often put the question aside, in order not to be embarrassed or confused by it.

But James has more to say:

> The truth is that your life has been for nothing unless you survive. Why should you go through all the difficulties and torments that everyone has to endure if there is no reason for it and no result from it, other than the perpetuation of the human race? Why should the species Man be continued at all, if he came from nowhere by chance coincidence and goes nowhere? To be extinguished like a light would mean that you remembered no more and suffered no more, it is true. But it would also mean that you nevermore knew joy and love.

The way I gained this type of philosophical information ostensibly from "the other side" was by what is termed automatic writing. Can you imagine how it feels to sit at your typewriter and have your fingers type information that your mind does not consciously instigate, that you don't even know? That is what I've been doing off and on for most of my life.

Naturally, I have questioned the source of the material, argued with it, and even fought with it. Does it really come, as it purports to, from surviving entities now residing in spirit dimensions of life? Or have I somehow tapped the universal unconscious—if there truly is such a thing? Might it be possible that my subconscious mind, with strange unfathomable powers, has gathered together brief bits from my (purposely) very limited reading of philosophical or occult literature; compiled, coordinated, reconstructed and embellished it with a great deal of additional information; and then poured it forth as automatic writing? To confound this theory is what three well versed Swedenborgians told me: a vast amount of the material written through me parallels exactly the accounts given in the eighteenth century by Emanuel Swedenborg, a Swedish metaphysician whose works I have never read.

In *Believe It or Not*, Robert Ripley said of Emanuel Swedenborg, "No single individual in the world's history ever encompassed in himself so great a variety of useful knowledge." The eminent scientist led a life largely devoted to studies covering practically the whole field of science. He traveled widely and was knighted by his queen for his achievements. He published volumes on mathematics, geology, chemistry, physics, mineralogy, astronomy and anatomy. This fantastic man gave up the study of worldly science at the age of fifty-six because he had become so psychic that he made daily trance visits into the spirit world—or so he believed. He wrote numerous works giving descriptions of the conditions he discovered there, and these became the basis for the Church of the New Jerusalem, which was founded after his death in 1772. Now without having the benefit of Swedenborg's information, since 1956 I have been receiving data very similar to his . . . which helps me accept my James's accuracy.

After I became housebound in my aching eighties, I was ready, even eager, to die (I wanted to see if all the information I believed I had been acquiring about the Hereafter was true). But I got so busy I didn't have time to die, thanks to the advent of Gary Schwartz and Linda Russek, authors of *The Living Energy Universe*. They have already introduced themselves professionally at the start of this book. Now it is my pleasure to describe them personally.

Gary looks like your basic wise college professor—neat beard, glasses—but in addition, he exudes an exceptional amount of inner warmth and caring.

Linda is brilliant, and she has a great figure. She really does look like a brunette Barbie doll. Who says academic types can't be gorgeous?

Early in our friendship they saw that, for a person who had led such an active life, I now had too much time on my hands. So they brought me a computer to keep me interested and interesting. As I learned to use the Windows software, the plan was that I would, through the Internet and e-mail, promote my codes widely. But it soon came to me that it would be wasted if I didn't write a book about my many years of effort to prove the survival of the human soul and all the activities that led to my decision to try to provide evidence by means of codes.

I said to Gary and Linda, "But if I write a thirtieth book, it will speak again about how I became interested in psychic phenomena and all the trials and traumas I went through trying to experience it. The goal of my life is my research and that is what I must reveal, but I'll have to repeat a lot that I've already told in some of my other books. Should I do that?"

Gary replied sweetly, "I hate to break it to you, Susy, but most of the people in the world have never read your books." I knew that!

Linda made it nice by adding, "And those who have read them will be eager to get more of the marvelous inspirational messages they provide."

So with that in mind, away we'll go down my personal yellow brick road, off to see the wizard (whose name is James). You'll hear of many new and strange things, but little more about the codes until the road leads ultimately to them in the last chapters. Most of my life has been a build-up to the exciting challenge of devising The Susy Smith Project Afterlife Codes Website and seeing its remarkable reception.

THREE

PREPARE YOURSELF
TO BE STUNNED

From the time I was twelve years old I have been trying
to find answers to life's eternal enigmas. I remember lying in
bed many nights during high school, praying—to whom I had
no idea—and then demanding hotly, "Oh, God, whoever or
whatever you are, please let me learn the truth!"

I was living in San Antonio during the years when I first
began to tackle the realities of existence—often sitting out
evenings in the yard under the Texas stars, which were really
as big and bright as the song says. Unfortunately, today's elec-
tricity has spoiled the night sky for city dwellers, but back
then the immensity of the universe was so startling, the
insignificance of man in relation to it so apparent, that I was
always wondering and always bewildered. What was especially
bemusing to me was the fact that everything in life has a definite origin and conclusion, an excuse for being and a reasonable explanation—everything, that is, except the greatest
and most profound questions of all.

It is interesting that this teenage girl who was pleading
with God for something to believe in that would make sense
to her has, after forty-four years of researching, found a philosophy that gives her and many of her readers some intelligent answers. Yet I fought it for years, applying every scientific

argument I was aware of as I floundered and suffered, and encountered many awkward situations—because what I was attempting was to rationalize communication with the spirits of the dead. It was an idea so far out that I had to challenge it, yet the material received from alleged spirits has been so much beyond anything my own mind could conceive that I am convinced it must come from some other source.

Eventually, I had to face the fact that nothing I had ever thought or conjectured could have produced anything so sensible, or in any possible way so inspiring, as the material that has flowed through my fingers when they are placed on the typewiter or computer keys loosely in the manner of communicating with spirits. How are you going to continue interminable arguing with statements like the following:

> Each human being is an original creation. From the moment of its inception in your body, your soul, or consciousness or spirit, lives forever. Man lives his life on Earth for one reason, and one reason only—to individualize himself and establish his identity and character. Creation continues eternally from the highest levels, entirely in accord with system and order. The consciousness that enters each unborn baby on the various inhabited planets of the universe comes from God (or divine consciousness or ultimate perfection; we use various names). Starting from life's experiences on Earth and continuing in spirit planes after he leaves through the transition of death, each individual is in a process of evolution, and he must eventually improve himself to the point of sublimity. Whatever progress is not made on Earth must be accomplished after death in spirit spheres of the universe. Ultimately each individual achieves unity from the highest, blissfully filling, because of his own special talents, capabilities, and individuality, a place which no other can fill in what might be called the Great Mosaic of Ultimate Perfection. In other words, the expanding universe is controlled by an expanding God

consciousness which is constantly increased by the addition of perfected human consciousnesses.

This concept never dawned on me as I was growing up. I was always a rationalist, never a credulous believer in anything since giving up Santa Claus, fairies and Sunday school. But you do not need to be a professional scientist to look at everything, yourself included, in an introspective and investigative manner. My lifetime, of course, has been right in the middle of what someone described as "that dark void of Godless intellectualism" that has gripped our civilization for so long. Thus I eventually decided that mental maturity was shown by disbelief in all the commonly accepted creeds.

I attended churches of almost every denomination in my early search for God, but most descriptions given of Him were unacceptable to me. Christians seemed to belittle their God by the way they interpret Him. Could a God with the love and intelligence to make a being who was shocked and horrified at the idea of eternal damnation have devised such a punishment Himself? Could God be any less compassionate than the kindest person who ever lived? In college a teacher said, "Man makes God in his own image." To me it seemed a most profound statement, and my agreement with it was my final step in becoming an agnostic.

Without an organized religion, I developed a philosophy of life that seemed adequate, behaving myself because it was sensible to conform to the mores of my era, not because I expected to win in the Hereafter (if there was one) any loving cups for achievement. I eventually brainwashed myself to the point that my slogan was "Always expect the worst and you won't be disappointed." And I wasn't disappointed: the worst always happened. I didn't have a very high opinion of life.

I believed that existence on Earth was unfair to most people and could have no excuse whatever without some kind of immortality where you could make up for what you had missed in life. No orthodox picture of immortality was acceptable to me, yet if anyone had even suggested taking any of the premises of spiritualism seriously, I'd have hooted. I stopped allowing myself conjectures of any kind, keeping my mind busy with reading, listening to music, oil painting, dancing and bridge. For roughly twenty years my quest for truth was sidetracked as I reached for any and every distraction to replace serious reflection.

My psychical research began when I was in my early forties. After becoming interested in it, I argued with it for years before finally allowing myself to admit that it was convincing. It is a difficult subject to be matter-of-fact about—and in truth many of its followers are dreamers or mystics—but there are few imaginative cells in my body, and I've always had a distinct aversion to superstition. Early on I discovered scientists at work in this area and learned from them how to observe each significant incident carefully and record it immediately.

Once beginning the research for the numerous books I have written about psychical phenomena, I became involved in all manner of weird occurrences. I have tracked ghosts to their lairs and bearded poltergeists in warehouses. I have been to pitch dark séances where the noisiest things were going on. I have traveled all over the United States and other countries. I have had a very interesting life.

But the main thing is that through my survival research and the enlightenment it has brought me, I have found faith in a God who gives me the opportunity to grow spiritually in an evolutionary process with glorious prospects. I've also found myself as well. What a great joy!

Although this book will tell of these and many other personal experiences, it is designed primarily to introduce the codes and our efforts through them to contact the Hereafter, and, also, to give my communicants' philosophy a good airing. Said James, who has provided most of my information:

I want here simply to give you this startling—to sophisticated contemporary people—idea that you do survive death and therefore that how you live on Earth is important. I will also of necessity try to show the reality of communication with those who have preceded you into the Afterlife and how to use the assistance we can offer you. Since we here are in the process of continual spiritual growth, we encourage you also to understand the need to forge ahead with your own personal development while you are still on Earth.

If you have knowledge of who you are and why you exist, you will have respect for yourself and for others, and you will be better able to adjust to the conditions of your world. When you understand that life is not just an accident, a cross one must bear for no logical reason if death brings extinction, that what you have believed on Earth is not the end of your progress in Heaven, then it will be possible for you to live more comfortably and think more successfully about yourself and your future in a life of eternal spiritual advancement.

Life is by no means an accident, but a design instead; and the design is so perfect that it almost stuns you when you realize it. Prepare yourself to be stunned!

FOUR

DON'T SING
BEFORE BREAKFAST

The kind of person I am was undoubtedly initiated by my Scotch and German forbears on my mother's side and my English and French-Canadian forbears on my father's. Unless some fey and romantic Scot slipped in there, my ancestors were probably all of relatively prosaic natures. There were no highwaymen that I know of, nor any mediums or psychics, but Daddy had a grandfather who fought in the American Revolution under Roger Williams, the founder of Rhode Island.

Mother was seventeen and Daddy twenty-five when they married. He was of medium height, a quiet man with a brilliant mind and a shy disposition. She was taller than he, vibrant and energetic, and had the most beautiful auburn hair you've ever seen. Mine was the same color when I was born, but it took tinting to keep it strawberry-blond when I got older. I got the green eyes that legitimately go with it, though.

Daddy was Merton M. Smith. Mother was Elizabeth Maude Anderson Hardegen Smith, a long name that came in handy when I later had to keep making her identify herself on the Ouija board. Yes, I used one of those when I first began trying spirit communication, but I don't recommend them because early on I discovered they carry a danger. More on that later.

I was named Ethel Elizabeth Smith. I wanted to be called Betty, Betsy or Beth, but Mother wouldn't hear of that because those were her names. So I went by the cold, crisp name of Ethel Smith, which always somehow sounded like a schoolteacher calling me down. Finally, during my college days, Daddy started teasing me with "Susy," a name which snuggled up to me warmly. After that I always told people my name was Susy, but now that I'm into a more scientific mode, I'm back to being Ethel Elizabeth from time to time. As for the last name, I'm a Smith who married a Smith. After my divorce, I was afraid another Smith would propose to me. I'd have been just fool enough to marry him, because it would have seemed funny to be the only three-time Smith in *The Guinness Book of World Records*. Of course, I'm safe from that now. It's too late to take on another man at my age and have to try to make husband material of him. It's all I can do now to learn to make this computer behave.

All these considerations pertain to what comes further on in my story. I was born in Washington, DC, on June 2, 1911. Halley's comet was traversing our planet's atmosphere at the time, and Mother would lie in bed at night holding me and watching it out her window. I always thought it would have been appropriate for me to have died when it appeared again in 1986. Longevity doesn't run in our family, and that would seem to have been long enough. But here I am, still around and kicking.

Let's begin by observing this little vessel known as Ethel on the potter's wheel of existence to learn if she will be shaped strongly enough to hold life's headiest potions without turning into a crackpot.

I was an only child, and we moved around so much I seldom got the chance to make good friends. This made adjustment difficult for me for a long time.

My lifelong habit of lonely peregrinations began when I was two. We were living in Front Royal, Virginia, where my father was chief clerk at the U.S. Army Remount Depot.

Mother came down with typhoid fever and Dad and I moved next door to a boarding house so we wouldn't catch it. I can remember—and it probably did intense and hidden things to my ego—crouching alone on a big, dark stairway there, my baby mind wondering what I had done that was so bad that my mother had gone off and left me.

Sensing my misery, Daddy took me to Baltimore to stay with friends until Mother was well. Characteristically, I bounced back from my initial unhappiness and was soon prolifically spouting Mother Goose rhymes, to the apparent edification of all concerned. In later years these friends loved to tell me how delighted they had been with me and how they had wanted to adopt me, but my father wouldn't hear of it when he came after six months and took me back to Front Royal.

At home was this strange, pale lady with no hair who wore fluffy white boudoir caps. Talk about your bright kids— I didn't even know my own mother! Still, I loved the lady in the white hat and wanted to be with her all the time, though I didn't recognize her until her hair grew back.

I was supposed to be precocious. In fact, a doctor warned Mother not to teach me anything in addition to what I was learning normally at the time, there being some current theory about it damaging a child's brain to learn too much too soon. As I grew older, the problems of social adjustment at school took care of my precocity.

My father was commissioned a captain in the army when I was six and soon we were transferred to Washington DC, where we lived in a boarding house until we could find a home of our own. Daddy almost immediately got pneumonia and pleurisy and was taken to Walter Reed Hospital with a temperature of a hundred-and-six degrees. He hadn't been there a week when Mother caught the flu. She was put into the room across the hall from him. I stood alone on the sidewalk in front of our lodgings and cried as they took Mother away in an ambulance. After a while I stopped crying, and my

17

main memory of the rest of that two-week period until Mother returned is that the twelve-year-old girl whose family ran the boarding house made me help her with the dishes every day, an imposition not lightly forgiven.

Convalescing after his near demise, my father was sent for a month's rest in Florida, and Mother came home from the hospital to find that I wasn't feeling so well myself. Within a few days I was down with something terrible in my throat. At first, the doctor thought it was laryngeal diphtheria, since I was choking to death. Another ambulance came and I, too, was taken to Walter Reed Hospital, just moments away from a tracheotomy. The doctors finally settled on a diagnosis of acute laryngitis and gave me steam inhalations all that night. These relieved the breathing problem, but I was left without any voice. As my quiet recovery began, there in that same hospital where my parents had just been favored patients, I got the royal treatment.

You see, if a child is ingenious enough she can achieve all the goodies her parents do!

From the material I have since received by automatic writing concerning the potency of the mind, I can readily see how my thoughts and intense unconscious desires worked to effect my illness. James is always very serious when he discusses the power of thought. To him, from his vast knowledge and experience, the mind is the strongest force in the world. It is particularly strong in its relationship with our own bodies.

"Many aspects of bodily function can be changed by your thinking," he said, "and you can be sick or well because of it."

Thus it seems logical to suspect that the numerous illnesses and operations throughout my life have been, at least in part, triggered by this original episode, when the height of achievement became the acquiring of some kind of disability that would get me to that same shrine where my parents had gone. My friend Bill Hanemann was later to say, "Susy goes to the hospital like anyone else goes to the supermarket."

Though it seems obvious to me now that my childhood trauma was partly responsible for this, in my twenties I also had a streptococcus blood poisoning, which led to many subsequent debilities, so my problems have not all been psychosomatic. But I know that until recently I was still unconsciously holding the concept of a hospital room as a nice, cozy place where nurses take care of you, doctors give you lots of attention, and you can retreat from the cares of the world. A womb with a view, you might say.

"Consciousness controls everything," James has written. He continues:

> All matter, which is composed of energy in a constant state of activity, is directed by mind, the overall regulating principle of the system through which it functions. If you consistently think positive, constructive thoughts, your anatomy tends to operate normally. Negative thoughts cause the opposite reaction. So keep yourself well by thinking happy thoughts and not causing your cells conflict.
>
> You can cure illnesses by the proper positive thinking because when you firmly believe that you are well, your body is motivated to begin to act that way. Watch yourself over a period of time and see if this is not true. There is nothing more effective for good than the constructive thoughts held strongly in your mind.

But most of us—in my generation at least—were programmed with all the old negative adages. My mother's Grandma used to say, "Don't sing before breakfast or you'll cry before supper," so Mother said it too. Although stoutly maintaining that I'm less superstitious than almost anybody, even today if I catch myself singing before breakfast, I stop. This is one instance where early indoctrination has stuck with me, no matter how hard I've tried in recent years to adopt James's and Norman Vincent Peale's positive thinking. It isn't easy to change the thought habits of a lifetime.

That's why my James is so set on starting youngsters out properly. He writes:

> If you would teach your small children, as soon as they learn to speak, to begin each day with an aphorism for health and happiness, their lives would be much more successful in every way. The child should learn to say each morning when he opens his eyes: "Today I will be healthy and happy all day long." Nothing else is necessary. He must learn to say it, not as a rote, but as an affirmation as important in the morning as his prayer at night. If he begins this very early, even before he can talk plainly, it will be such a part of his life's pattern that he will not think of it as a chore but as a normal routine. His life will be immeasurably improved because of it.

James is undoubtedly right, and it will be easier for children raised this way to conquer the vicissitudes of the world because of their positive attitude. But what about those of us who didn't have the opportunity to learn it in our youth? Even after I read Dr. Norman Vincent Peale's book on the subject— *The Power of Positive Thinking*—and consciously tried to practice it, I had no luck. Now James was going on the same way.

"It's easy enough for you to propound these fine phrases," I complained to my invisible associate after a few futile efforts to practice his teachings. "But just plain folks like me are the ones who have to do it, and you haven't made it a bit clear how we're supposed to go about it."

James's reply was immediate:

> You consciously deny every negative thought that comes into your mind and substitute a positive one for it. Do not make a big issue of the denial. A negative thought repressed is harmful. Merely toss it out, instead; then substitute a positive thought in its place. For "I can't do that, it's too difficult," think, "That's untrue, of

course I can do it, and I'll be successful." This might not sound as sensible as it really is, but try it. You will discover that it works. That's the important thing—it works!

We must not only deny each negative thought that appears, but we should prepare ourselves for such thoughts in advance by a daily recital of constructive aphorisms. James suggests, "Start every day with the statement that you are a brilliant, stimulating mind living in a healthy, normally functioning body. Let no negative reaction deny this as the day goes forward, and occasionally repeat the statement."

We will achieve much more with all our efforts to live successfully if we will only learn this, he says. No one need be poor or unhappy (at least, not for long), no matter how hopeless your case may seem. But you won't be successful without effort. You have to practice positive thinking as diligently as you would practice the violin if you wish to become a virtuoso. It's entirely up to you whether or not you want to bother with it.

"Those who wish to live so that they will have a more successful life on Earth and a head start in future planes of existence have only so to decide," James states. "When you make up your mind that you will expend the effort to keep your life in a constructive path and maintain your thoughts under control, you will learn to do so. While it is very hard work, it is no more difficult than to give up a bad habit or to learn a new aptitude."

I must say James convinced me. I've spent a number of years now trying to practice what he preaches, and circumstances have definitely changed for the better in my life. Too bad it came so late or I probably could have conditioned myself to consistently better health as well.

There's no doubt that the little six-year-old tyke lying there in Walter Reed Hospital unable to talk could have had a more successful life in every way if she'd known about such things. While convalescing, I was sitting up in bed reading Charles and

Mary Lamb's *Tales of Shakespeare* and basking in the nurses' "oh's" and "ah's" of surprise at how "bright" I was. I was ready, though not eager, to go home in a week . . . without my voice. It wasn't recaptured for a year, but even at that young age I was not the strong silent type, so I never gave up trying to talk, especially since I started several new schools during that period and felt self-conscious without speech. When my sound box did gradually begin functioning again, I forced it constantly, with the result that I've had a husky voice ever since, which carries into all the places it is not supposed to go.

The year I couldn't talk, my father was Quartermaster at Ft. Sill, Oklahoma. Because of my illness, Mother and I did not go with him. Later we took the train to Indianapolis to visit Mother's sisters. It was the first time they had reunited since their childhood, and we enjoyed being near them so much that we never did go back to Washington. When Dad joined us, we bought a home and stayed put. But then my globe-trotting father was sent to the Philippines—a long and lonely way from Indiana. I was the wrong age for my cousins to take me up, and Mother wasn't one to go out socially, so we rattled around in the big house alone. I pulled my nose out of books occasionally to play with paper dolls, for whom I loved to draw dresses. Mother kept busy at her sewing machine, but we were disheartened dullards, just the two of us alone.

Luckily, Aunt Ivy had a friend, a tiny woman named Nina Sharpe, who was recently divorced and looking for a place to live. She moved into our home and into our hearts. We never let her leave us again, and she became a miniature second mother to me. A graduate of the Indianapolis Conservatory of Music, Nina showed me what the piano had been designed for, playing wonderful classical music for us whenever we asked her.

"I want to play wonderful classical music, too," I told her, so she started giving me lessons. But the simple exercises, which had to be practiced endlessly, were so boring that I gave them up as a bad job. My musical education has continued only as a receptive listener (I am passionate about almost every kind of music) and my artistic urges were played out in writing and painting, for which I have considerably more patience and aptitude.

During our three years in Indianapolis, to make up for the taunts I got in school that "Ethel swallered the dictionary," I tried to be an exceptionally good outdoor scout (away from Mother's supervision), doing anything daredevilish and adventurous. The neighborhood boys and I coasted our sleds off high banks or slid them over the frozen pond nearby. We ran all over the highest scaffolding on the apartment buildings under construction, playing "follow the leader," swinging from pipe to pipe in the basement like monkeys, and jumping from porch roofs into sandpiles. Once I fell when trying to leap from a high pile of bricks to the top of a shed. I landed on my back on the sidewalk, but even that didn't stop my career of "good sportsmanship."

The Smiths found the Pacific Ocean getting wider with the passing months, so Daddy, now a major at last, resigned and came home. Reentering government service in the Agricultural Department, he was almost immediately sent to Salt Lake City.

Mother was firm about it this time. "We're going with you," she said, and she put our house up for sale. I pored over pictures of Utah in the geography books, eager for an idea of what mountains and desert were like. But it took nearly a year to sell the house. By then my father had been transferred to San Antonio, Texas. That's where we finally caught up with him.

The beauty of the flowers and trees of semitropical San Antonio enchanted us. I think every child should be raised in sunshine and warmth so he can expand and bloom like a rose. But with my usual nonchalance, I got sick soon after we got there. The doctor thought things in my interior had been scrambled by my porch-climbing fall in Indianapolis. I was put to bed for a year so that they could arrange themselves back in order. This wasn't the intolerable hardship it might

23

sound like. Nina—she was part of the family now so naturally she went to Texas with us—brought me books from the library when she came home from work, and nobody called me away from an exciting chapter to do the dishes. Books like *Graustark* and *The Prisoner of Zenda* were my favorites, and I evolved from them a very refined (and unrealistic) idea of romantic love with which to begin my teens.

Returning to school the next year, I was a class behind; it was still difficult to adjust to my peers, particularly boys, though I'd always enjoyed their company before and they liked me in return. Why, I was even engaged at six to a boy in Washington named Jerome. (That terminated abruptly when he hit me on the head with a rock.) Now all this was changed, and it was years before I grew to be at ease again with the more exciting sex. Oh, the unendurable longings of an undesired teenager! My ardent aim was to be a blasé sophisticate like the older girls, who were known as "flappers," but I couldn't make the grade.

As the twenties roared out, I was roaring into my teens equipped with all the wrong things. I had a blossoming bosom when it was the style to be flat as a pecan praline. I had none of the easygoing, slangy banter necessary to communicate with the manly "sheiks" I wanted to impress. This seems strange because I was quick with a quip, but never (it seemed to me) at the right time or place. Analyzing my every remark at home later, I was sure I'd said the wrong thing on every possible occasion.

And Mother wouldn't let me wear lipstick! That was the crowning indignity. Inferiority complexes were frequently spoken of in those days, and mine was a biggie. What I've always been, let's face it, is an introverted extrovert.

Thus, when my high school annual contained the caption under my senior class picture, "A future artist, a girl with talents in many directions and a likeable disposition," it made no encouraging impression on me. Nothing had encouraged me much all the way through high school.

I finished the whole thing off with a flourish of measles, missing most of the graduation ceremonies and parties.

FIVE

MOSTLY ABOUT MEN

The University of Texas was a friendly campus—known as the Forty Acres. My favorite memory of it was the many large beds of poppies intermingled with pastel larkspur that bloomed all over in the spring.

In college I majored in men. Journalism was ostensibly my main subject, but dates took precedence over everything else, including grades. I had made the honor roll continuously in high school, but never had any fun. Now I made up for lost time. I was engaged to Jack the first year, Richie the second year—and then came Henry, who was big and handsome and seemed extra special. Every weekend toward the close of that school year we would almost run away and get married, but sanity would prevail when I returned to the dorm at night and begged the girls to talk me out of it. But we put it off once too often, and eventually other priorities intervened.

We had firmly decided that we were going to get married right after school let out for the summer and then go to Colorado to work on a goldmine Henry had grubstaked the previous year. When we went to my home in June, however, my father was desperately ill with malignant hypertension—the highest of high blood pressure. The family hadn't told me how bad he was because they didn't want to worry me, and I'd been so immersed in Henry that I hadn't been home for ages.

Daddy was still able to spend a little time at his office, but the doctor had forbidden him to drive. I was expected to use my summer chauffeuring him back and forth to work.

"But I'm going to get *married!*" I wailed.

Daddy called me by the nickname he'd begun using lately. "I need you, Susy," he said.

So Henry went off to Colorado alone, and I stayed home and wrote daily letters to him. When he received my frantic SOS late in August, he started hitchhiking to reach me, and I didn't hear from him for two agonizing weeks. He finally arrived in September, just a few days before my father died.

I hadn't believed anyone close to me could die. I'd never seen death before, being an only child in a traveling tribe that had never been intimate enough with other families to attend their funerals. I hadn't realized it, but death terrified me. Then the dreaming began and made it worse. I had horrible nightmares every night that we'd buried Dad and he came back, or that he sat up in his coffin at his funeral and told us he was still alive. Or even that we'd buried him alive. Frequently, I'd jump out of bed screaming, sure that a luminous figure had been standing beside me.

With my usual efforts to analyze myself and my reactions, I evaluated the dreams as caused by a guilty conscience because I had been so much more concerned about Henry's being away than about my father's illness. Now it seems to me more likely that my father, after his death, was trying to get through to me in my sleep that he was really still alive and wanting me to know it. If this were true, he must have eventually realized that, because of my half-reception of his messages (which my subconscious was distorting into something monstrous in the dreams) he was doing me more harm than good. So he stopped his efforts, but not until he had broken up my romance with Henry—fortunately.

Henry and I went back to our fourth year of college, but we didn't get along very well. My ragged nerves caused by the dreams aggravated Henry's argumentative disposition, which aggravated *my* argumentative disposition. Our constant bickering made me more querulous and him more bossy. Finally we decided on a dramatic separation, hoping that absence would make our hearts grow fonder, like in the movies. At midterm I went to the University of Arizona, where I'd spent a semester once before, but it wasn't possible to concentrate on either lessons or dates with other boys, so I soon gave up and came home. After our big and happy reunion, Henry and I began fighting again. This time Mother came to the rescue with an extended vacation trip. She and Nina and I got into our little Ford and took off for the north and the east to visit friends and relatives.

Several months later, while we were in Detroit visiting my father's sister Mabel, I heard through the grapevine that my Henry had married another. Heart torn to minced tenderloin, I decided to get an office job and remain in Detroit, where I could go into my decline far away from the prying eyes of Texas.

I didn't decline for long, because Aunt Mabel's son Stan introduced me to his friend M. L. (nicknamed "Memo" or "Mo") Smith. We were married within two months. I soon discovered that Mo's soft brown eyes, which sometimes sparkled, more often shot off sparks instead.

Still, nothing was going to keep me from having an award-winning marriage. Never admitting to myself that things were seldom congenial, I set about learning to be a good housewife. It took a bit of doing, because all I knew how to cook were cakes and fudge. But my cakes always fell in the unpredictable oven of our apartment, and Mo didn't care for fudge. His technique of showing disapproval was to stop speaking, sometimes for as long as a week. I remember the third morning we were married, this absentminded wife pouring him a cup of hot water from the coffeepot. He didn't speak for the rest of the day. I never knew what to do in response. Just feeling hurt or crying got no results. If I tried not to talk either, I almost exploded. It turned out that the only way to get around his silence was for me to go into such a violent rage that he would have to soothe me to quiet me down. Then we'd start laughing and begin to do married-people kinds of things. I acquired a stevedore's vocabulary and rather enjoyed the outbursts, making a real production of them. But I had to unlearn the whole routine at a later time to get my former good disposition back.

We had been enduring marriage together for a year and a half when we decided to take a Texas vacation in August. I became very ill on the trip with streptococcus septicemia—the most virulent form of blood poisoning. By the time we reached Mother in San Antonio, I was almost comatose, with a low-grade fever that kept me lying in bed without stirring or eating for two weeks.

Then the infection localized in my left hip and the pain became so intense that I screamed whenever the joint was moved. I was taken to the hospital and put in a plaster cast. I tried to pray that night, the first real praying I'd ever done in my life. The attack of religion didn't last past the illness, but it carried me through—along with the prayers of those who loved me. A neighbor, Bonnie Pitman, kissed me good-bye when I was taken to the hospital. After my return home she told me the good-bye had been for real, because the doctor had said I had no more than one chance in a thousand to pull through. This was in the days before the discovery of sulfa drugs and penicillin, so it was a miracle that I survived at all.

When I went home from the hospital I was laid out flat in a fracture bed, with a cast that started at my waist and went to my ankle on the left leg, to my knee on the right. I would have to stay in it three months and it would stiffen the left hip joint so it wouldn't bend. Unbeknownst to me then, I'd be lame for the rest of my life.

My days in the cast weren't too bad; *Gone with the Wind* had just come out and Nina read it aloud to me. When she stopped reading the last chapter to help prepare dinner, I grabbed the book and held it up in the air over my head to finish it. Then I cried buckets of tears because I knew that Clark Gable was Rhett Butler, and I couldn't stand Scarlett being so mean to him. I passed the time after that knitting an afghan, holding my hands up in the air as with the book.

Nights were most difficult. Mo never came home until very late. He claimed to be working at a job he had taken in order to stay in Texas with me. When I found out later he had been playing woof-woof with a girl instead, I got a divorce.

The next year I had an arthroplasty, a hip operation in which they attempted to make a new joint. It was not quite successful, but after that I got along fairly well using a cane for support. As I started my convalescence, Mother was selling our San Antonio house so that we could return to the old family home she had just inherited in the small resort town of Oakland, in the mountains of Western Maryland. Mother and Nina planned to rent rooms to tourists in the area.

We arrived to find a decrepit, doddering old house, all of whose nine rooms plus exterior needed every possible rejuvenating trick to revive them. Betty Smith, my energetic mother, considered it a personal challenge, and she directed a crew of carpenters as they roofed, plastered, papered, puttied and painted. Even when the workmen were finished, she was still building shelves and cupboards, along with shoveling snow in the winter as she particularly loved to do. Unfortunately, she was putting more pressure on her weak heart than she realized.

I occupied myself reading, oil painting and doing anything else that didn't take much physical effort. I was on crutches for two years, and it took over four to recuperate fully from the hip surgery. Though I'd had a successful restoration of motion, the infection had eaten away so much of the bone that there was only a very shallow hip socket and a tiny femur head left, which did not even fit in the socket but sat at the outside edge of it, somehow held in place only by scar tissue and muscle. The support of a cane continued to be needed when walking, but a cane really isn't so bad once you've made friends with it.

To move this book along to my psychic experiences, I should pass quickly over periods of deep emotion. But how can I, without seeming maudlin, go into the thoughts of a person in her twenties suddenly facing the fact that her life would henceforth be compelled to move at a considerably slower pace? I still thought of myself as a rather diverting young thing, yet one day I overhead a little boy walking by the house say to his companion, "This is where that crippled woman lives." To see ourselves as others see us can be an anguish not easily rendered in words.

Still, my friends professed to think of me as Susy, one of whose small conceits was that she affected a walking stick. Who can object to that?

SIX

SUSANNA DON'T YOU CRY

At first Mother, Nina and I delighted in experiencing the changing seasons again in Maryland. The trees on the mountains flamed red and gold in autumn and the snows in winter were exhilarating. We found that these two stayed much too long, however. Spring cried the whole time it was there, and summer hardly smiled at all. I spent the next nine years trying to figure out how to get back to the South.

Yet it was nice to live in a small town while convalescing, for it was much easier to get around and I relished the new experiences offered. I fooled around there in Oakland for several years without accomplishing much more than getting better and having a moderately good time. Then Daddy's insurance money ran out and I contemplated having to leave home to go to work. I was always contemplating leaving home for one reason or another, because, much as I loved Mother, she had never noticed that I was grown and continually kept trying to run my life for me. She even told me which spoon to stir the gravy with and exactly how to thread my needles. I guess this is typical mother stuff, but it irked me.

My dear friend Mary Elliott, who, with her four little kids, was a delight to me then and is the main reason I've enjoyed visiting Oakland over the years since, told me once, "You know, Susy, you never really matured until your mother died."

She was right. But it wasn't for lack of trying.

I contacted the Maryland Vocational Rehabilitation Service for job placement, and they kindly got me what seemed like an excellent position in Baltimore—secretary to the director of nursing at one of the newest hospitals. My shorthand was never very good, but my knowledge of medical terms and hospital routines was excellent, and so I was well-enough qualified. Unfortunately, it was one of the most trying experiences of my life, due to the arrogance of the head nurse. In fact, it turned out that they had hired a person from out of town just because of her. Her reputation was so bad, no local would take the job. Nonetheless, I stuck it out for nearly a year.

Once during this time, hoping I could learn to adjust to this woman, I went to see a psychiatrist. It turned out he wore a hearing aid, and I felt I had to holler my innermost secrets at him. He finally asked about my dreams, and I said innocently, "Well, the other night I dreamed about a boa constrictor."

"Get married, young lady. Anyone can get married," he replied, and quickly ushered me out the door. Years later, when I told a friend my story about the psychiatrist who wore a hearing aid, he whooped with laughter. "You know what snakes meant to Freud?" he asked. "And you had to say, of all things, a boa constrictor!"

That's how I do things—wholeheartedly.

So I got the mumps. Where was I after they slunk away? Right back home in Oakland, convalescing again.

Concerning James's admonition about the power of thought, I don't know how I got the mumps out of thin air when no one was ill around me. But if ever I secretly wanted to run home to Mommy, this was it. So did I make it happen the hard way, by getting sick? Maybe. I don't want to overdo it, though, because I've been sick one way or another all my life, while having a very active joy of living whenever conditions would behave themselves.

Finally, I was lucky enough to find fascinating work right at home. The Mountain Democrat newspaper had been closed down during the war. When it reopened they hired me as a reporter. One thing or another had always kept me from practicing my college journalism, but it was still my goal. It became evident during my three years there that with my gregarious nature, newspaper work was what I'd been designed for.

I soon learned to know a large percentage of Garrett County and was invited to nearly every meeting, banquet and luncheon that occurred. (Small-town newspaper people are a well-fed crowd.) I wrote everything from front page news stories to personals, weddings and funerals; there was even a *Shopping with Susy* column that was quite popular. I also did makeup of the front page when the editor was sick, and helped run the press on publication day. This was the first challenging work I had ever undertaken. I thrived on it. I also acquired an enduring love for the "dear hearts and gentle people" in that only small town of my experience.

But, oh, those winters in the Maryland mountains were cold! I was plodding my rounds through snow and ice, dressed in ski pants, sweaters, fur coat, fleece-lined boots, fur-lined gloves, wool head scarf, ear muffs—sometimes even red flannel longies. I was constantly in fear that my cane would skid and flatten me and I'd have to do another stretch in casts and hospitals.

I yearned for warmer climes, but Mother was becoming increasingly ill, so I could do no more than secretly dream of leaving.

In 1947 Mother gave me a musical powder box for Christmas, which played "Susanna Don't You Cry." But even though it admonished me not to, every time I raised its lid and heard the tinkly tune, I cried anyway, because I knew by then that Mother was dying, and hearing that melody always called attention to the fact.

After working overtime wrestling with the big old house for eight years, Mother's heart had begun to fail rapidly. She was satisfied that she'd lived an active life to its fulfillment, but now she was bedridden, with her difficulty in breathing causing the most discomfort. Nina and I gave her devoted care, and there was one compensation in it for me—for the first time in my life, I could do things for my mother in return for all the affection she had given me.

She was never cross, never complaining, even though all during her last year she sat in bed and gasped for breath. She wasn't afraid to die, confident she was only being separated from us for a while, but to me that assurance was groundless. It was nice that Mother and Nina had faith but it was no help to me. I had no belief in a Hereafter.

Mother waited until spring to die, leaving us on the twenty-first of March, two months before her sixtieth birthday. That day she told us she wanted to be taken by train back to San Antonio so she could be buried beside my father, and so that Nina and I would have a few weeks to be among our Texas friends there. She even made jokes on the day she left us—little efforts to raise our spirits—and as we gently teased with her, we found her bravery inspiring. That afternoon I sat beside her on her bed as we played a game of cribbage. She beat me.

Her last words to us were thanks for the loving care we had given her. Then she said, "I wish someone would tell me where I am," and then, "Don't leave me." And then she was gone.

My little music box had sat on my dresser neglected for months because of the tears its tune brought to my eyes every time it played. Now it stayed at the house while Nina and I took Mother to Texas for burial and two weeks of visiting.

About four o'clock one morning, shortly after our return to Maryland, the powder box began to play. I woke up alarmed, then somehow comforted, at the strains of "Oh, Susanna, don't you cry for me." It seemed momentarily like a direct message from Mother, but I almost immediately began trying to figure some natural means by which the lid could have jarred itself loose. There were no vibrations in the house, we did not have mice—what else could have caused it? That I wasn't able to conceive of how it happened did not

convince me it was anything other than a physical phenomenon, free of any supernatural origin. But what you profess to
believe and what you secretly hope could be true are two different things. It was consoling at least to consider the possibility that Mother was using this means to tell me she was still
around.

I was too pushed by business to spend much time pondering it, however, being involved in my first attempt at super-
salesmanship. Oakland was to have its centennial that summer, and the minute Nina and I returned from Texas, the
committee had asked me to take charge of selling $8,000
worth of advertising for the centennial program. I'd make a
good commission and be able to occupy my mind, so the
opportunity pleased me.

Trading in Mother's small car for a bigger one, I drove
every day to Cumberland, Baltimore, Pittsburgh, or other
neighboring cities, selling $50 ads here, $25 ads there, $100 ads
another place, and after nearly three busy months, sales went
over the top.

Then the centennial was over. Oakland settled back into
its routines and Susy struggled out of her rut, as impatient as
a whistling teakettle to flee away South.

"You'll have to go alone. I can't possibly leave my piano
pupils," Nina told me, for she had music classes she delighted in. We turned half the house into an apartment and rented it so she would have company. Then I packed my car with
all my favorite personal possessions—even a chairside phono-
graph and several hundred classical record albums—and hied
me away to Florida to sit under a coconut tree.

SEVEN

WORKING IN AN
AMIABLE MADHOUSE

My first three years in Florida were a period in which I learned to face life without any kind of parental domination, and it was good for me. With no Mother to run home to when things got tough, I had to square up to each situation and make my own decisions, for better or worse, and I responded adequately. I had loved Mother. She was the most wonderful person I'd ever known. But I welcomed the challenge of trying to make it on my own. There were many problems and lots of grievances in doing it, and the results could hardly be called successful, but neither did they signify failure.

Back in mockingbird country once again, I rejoiced as their melodious tunes made merry with the atmosphere. The blue ocean sparklingly invited me for a dip. The glistening palm trees suggested I sit for a while in their shade and the sunshine begged me to bask in its warmth. I cooperated fully. The look and feel and sounds of the Sunshine State made me happy, and it was the first time happiness had lived with me in a long while.

I applied for a newspaper job in every city I came to while touring the state, but in September of 1949 nothing was going on in Florida except the autumnal equinox, and nobody was hiring anybody. I eventually ended up back on Florida's east coast, in Daytona Beach, selling radio advertising and putting on a program called *Shopping with Susy*.

I also learned to be "mommy" to a new puppy. I'd discovered that living alone wasn't to my liking. I needed someone to wag his tail when I came home evenings.

Fortunately, just two months before, a miniature dachshund had been born with the intention of becoming mine, so when I went to the kennel, he immediately stuck his head out of the basket of rolling, tumbling puppies and claimed me. I picked him up—the pee-wee of them all—and said, "I'll take this one. He's a redhead, too, and it's the style for dogs to have owners to match."

From then on, wherever I went, the little sausage named Junior wobbled and spilled along beside me. He helped me to sell advertising, for even people who find it easy to resist a woman salesperson can melt to jelly over a dachshund pup. The little fellow would be my constant companion for twelve years, yet who could dream that after his death he would become the object of one of my most compelling psychic experiences?

About three months after I went to Daytona Beach, my radio job was terminated because I just couldn't leave the ocean alone. Beachcombing is an occupational hazard of the tropics. In Daytona one drives one's car on the flat beach, and I'd route myself via the ocean when making my business calls around town. The piled-up clouds, the festoons of flying pelicans and the capering waves were so irresistible that I simply had to frolic with them on my lunch hour. It was one of the most delightful episodes of my life, that balmy first spring in Daytona, as I floated on my back, rolling with the "slow swinging seas," as much a part of the ocean life as the porpoise scalloping his way through the water.

The radio station manager wasn't happy when I came in late from lunch because of my swims, and working evenings to make up for it didn't seem to appease him. So we got into a little discussion, and then I went away without a job.

At the time I had only $300 in the bank and a puppy to support; nonetheless I began to think seriously about starting a shopping guide. It would be a free throwaway sheet, to be paid for by the advertising. Every merchant I approached encouraged me, seeming to think there was money to be acquired that way. I figured to have fun and make a good living, being able to work the hours I chose and have time for the beach, too.

The only one of those dreams that came true was the fun. *That* I had. The light of experience now indicates that my health and my pocketbook would have survived in better shape if such a taxing enterprise had never been started. Had hindsight been foresight, I wouldn't have had the nerve to begin. All I knew then was that I could write ads and sell them, that I got along well with people and that the merchants of Daytona said they needed a shopping guide. What more was required?

I soon found out, as I coped with social security and withholding tax, making collections from tough accounts, cutthroat maneuvers from would-be competitors, hiring and firing employees, struggling with the most uncooperative machine ever invented—a typesetter that (supposedly) aligned type into columns—and trying to produce acceptable radio programs on a tape recorder whose tapes were the wrong width to be played over the studio equipment (no one at the radio station could identify the problem). Yes—eventually there was a radio program in addition to the weekly paper.

From its initial issue, *Shopping with Susy* was a success with readers, if not with the bank. (This was during a period when all of Florida was in the doldrums.) It was a nice-looking tabloid-sized sheet, six pages thick at first, although later it went up to twelve and fourteen pages during rush seasons. It was written with the lightest possible touch—interesting sidelights about the advertisers and jokes and stories that had a local application. It had a different appeal from most shopping guides because of its manner of gently ribbing advertisers, readers and ourselves as well. It was (we thought) fresh and bright, and certainly no one ever knew just what to expect from it or what we were likely to come up with next.

Although we soon went to offset as the easier way to handle production, *Shopping with Susy* was at first printed at a small independent newspaper shop. The foreman, Bill Beard, had a large black bull terrier named Lil, of whom Junior, my dachshund, was very fond, and watching the big black dog and the small red puppy romping together became part of our daily routine.

One day when Junior was about five months old, Bill came storming into my office waving the mat of a picture I had asked him to cast in metal so that it could be reproduced in my paper. It was of a black soldier returning home from the Korean War. Bill, who had been reared in South Carolina a long time ago, threw the mat onto my desk and demanded to know why I was putting a picture of a "nigger" in my paper.

"If he's good enough to fight for us, he's certainly good enough to have his picture published," I said. "We'll run it proudly."

"Well, I won't set it." said Bill, and he left it on my desk.

A little later I took the mat back to the shop and handed it to him, but he still refused to have anything to do with it. Then I got mad.

My pup was at that moment wagging his tail vigorously at Lil and rubbing noses with her.

"Come, Junior," I said, snatching him from the floor. "A nice little red dog like you is too good to play with that *black* dog."

And I stormed out.

Bill Beard cast the picture.

Shopping with Susy grew so large, so fast, that another writer had to be hired, then another salesgirl. Next, to protect the paper from its editor's legerdemain (I'd been keeping the records with a clever little triple-entry system of my own devising) the next logical step was to employ a bookkeeper.

If the staff was soon almost too big for me to handle, it was also competent and charming, and several of the girls who worked there have remained fond friends over the years. They sold ads, wrote copy and pasted up the dummy of the paper that went to the photo-offset printer each week, frequently working until two or three in the morning on the night before press day. And later, when I got sick—don't I always?—they took care of me and in general were family.

In addition, as main contributor to our wit, humor and entertainment, we had the late, enchanting Bill Hanemann. I will go into some detail about him, because several years later he was to become chief confidant, pepper-upper, and ghost-chaser when I returned to Daytona Beach with a house trailer full of spooks in tow.

As a nonconformist, satirist, and debunker, Bill Hanemann was another H. L. Mencken. He was a practicing individualist, to the point of wearing a bristly moustache and riding a bicycle to work long before they were in style, and doing anything else that occurred to him anywhere he happened to be when the notion struck him, but everyone put up with all his peculiarities because he was so much fun. With his short, stocky figure and his deep husky voice, he was the most masculine of men, but he often wore a beret in an area of the country where berets were looked on with suspicion. I can remember going into stitches once when we were waiting in line for ice cream cones at a Dairy Queen and Bill decided to illustrate some point we were discussing about the Swan Lake ballet. Entirely oblivious to the curious stares of passersby, he performed several intricate dance steps, almost graceful in his tennis shoes.

Bill and his gracious wife, Helen, ran the Marigold House restaurant, but he still found time to bestow on us his brilliant commentary, in the form of editorials much too good for our small effort. He did this, he said, not just because he approved of the paper, but because I allowed him to write what he wanted to. (Though what he wrote always had to be cooled down, with great argument between us, because he was also ahead of his time in what he thought could appear in print.) Since he used to be a successful script writer in Hollywood—Fred Astaire's *Flying Down to Rio,* no less, was one of his—all his largess had a polish and style that lifted the paper into a higher literary bracket.

Shopping with Susy became very popular around town and we soon started the companion radio program. Its theme song, "If You Knew Susy," played before and after the show. The paper and the program grew so well-known that whenever I walked into a local nightspot, the pianist or band would immediately start playing "my song." I cherished this attention. Realizing that most of it was in hopes that in a return of professional courtesy, I'd emphasize in the paper the latent genius of the entertainer, I usually did so.

People knew my face from the picture on the masthead, my voice from the radio, Junior (our mascot) because he "wrote" a column in the paper and even my car because it was decked with little *Shopping with Susy* signs fore and aft. Whenever they saw us, they whistled and waved, and I waved back, loving every minute of it.

I didn't have a bad social life, either. For a while I took pleasure in running with the Florida wolf pack—until I learned that in that vacationers' paradise, "single" meant that your wife didn't make the trip with you. Then I settled down to a few old standby friends, and very few dates. But the paper kept me so occupied that I didn't mind.

Shopping with Susy never did make any money. If our advertisers had paid proper attention to the bills we sent them, we would have been solvent, but unhappily, too many small businesses in Daytona at that time were in the same leaky lifeboat. I had due bills at all the dress shops and restaurants that advertised, so I took their ad payment out in trade. I wore lovely clothes and ate dinner every night in style. Later I mortgaged the family home in Maryland to give the paper a financial transfusion. Then survive our little newspaper did, with banner heads held high—for a while longer.

Even with all our problems, we had much hilarity. *Shopping with Susy* was more like a party than a business, and my home, in which we worked, was more like a clubhouse than an office. I'm afraid Bill Hanemann's description of it as an "amiable madhouse" wasn't too far from the truth. It's certain that no one ever knew when arriving there if he'd get a kiss, a bat on the head, a Scotch and soda, or a peanut butter sandwich. So, it was also referred to as a salon of distinction, because of the diverting people who congregated there.

EIGHT

WHO SAID PIONEERING
DAYS ARE OVER?

It took a long spell of illness to convince me. I didn't think it would be possible to live without *Shopping with Susy*, but I finally learned I couldn't live *with* it. Doctors said that apparently, the pressures I worked under brought my strep infection back in some low-grade form they couldn't identify. For months I was in and out of the hospital and lived on sulfa, penicillin, cortisone and every known antibiotic. Sometimes they'd make my temperature cool off, but it always heated up again soon, and I ached all the time.

Most of the newspaper work fell upon the staff, and those wonderful people not only kept the paper running but prepared and served my meals, did the marketing and even sometimes the housework. After awhile this seemed to me just too much of an imposition on them, and even though they didn't complain, I did. So I sold the paper, with tears in my eyes. I only got $300 for it, but since that was exactly what had been put into it in the first place, it could be said that the deal came out even.

What to do with myself now? It was the early 1950s, and no one in Daytona Beach had ever heard of auto races. Without the paper Daytona was no pleasure to me, and anyway, it was too damp for my particular condition. I wanted to get dry enough to dehydrate like a piece of Melba toast, but I didn't know where to go.

Just in the nick of that time of indecision, the estate of the last of my great aunts was settled and I inherited $5,000. With this grubstake I decided to break camp and go West. My thoughts frequently being father to my actions, Junior and I were on our way in a short time, eventually ending up in the desert country of Southern California.

Moving into a small efficiency cottage, I hibernated, seeing almost no one, spending my days relaxing in the sunshine and hoping the desert air would make me well. Unfortunately, my problems were not climate-curable. My doctor in neighboring Palm Springs couldn't find anything wrong other than a cyst on my thyroid gland, and he didn't think that was the cause of my temperature elevation and shortness of breath; however, he stated, it had to come out sometime, because it would never go away of its own accord and might become malignant.

Finally one day I said to him, "Look, if you don't cut my throat, I will."

So he did.

I got along fine, but still found it all rather discouraging. I told my surgeon, "All my girlfriends go to the hospital and return with babies. I go more than anybody and all I ever have to show for it is scars. And most of *them* I can't properly show!"

"I've got news for you, Susy," he responded. "You might as well prepare yourself for another scar you can't show, and that very soon." Then he explained that their thorough checkup had revealed the necessity of another operation somewhat further south of my thyroid. Within a month I had that done, too; and there among numerous large cysts and fibroid tumors was a little pocket of endometriosis—*that* was the seat of many of my current problems. After all that surgery, I felt wonderful for years.

Convalescing in my desert retreat, however, was purely lonely. Existence began to seem as parched as the wastelands around me as I lay about doing nothing more stimulating than healing and reading. No phones ringing every five minutes. No people dropping in constantly to talk. No men. No nothing.

My thoughts dwelt so much on the fun of *Shopping with Susy* that I decided to write a book about it; I began spending all my time at my typewriter.

Junior was also busy. He whiled away his hours hanging around the yard chasing little lizards. Reptiles do not have a personality one can snuggle up to, and I prefer them to keep their distance. In fact, I rather insist upon it. But my dog loved his life there.

Have you ever been all alone in the desert with nobody to talk to but a dachshund and an occasional chuckwalla? If so, you can probably see why the thought of home and friends began to creep nostalgically into my mind more often than not. I told Junior that if my boredom ever came to the point where I felt like joining him in his lizard hunts, we'd go back to Nina in Maryland. And one day in late March, just a month after my last operation, I actually found myself wandering out in the sand with the dog, saying, "There's one, see him? There he goes, under that greasewood bush!"

We packed up three days later and started back east.

Nina and the big old house were glad to see us, even though I turned traitor to the house immediately by putting a "For Sale" sign on it. But it took a year and a half to sell, because my price was too high.

When the time came that our home would be sold, Nina and I both would have to settle somewhere. I had no means of making a living in the little town in the Maryland mountains (the *Democrat* had closed) and for that matter, I was still obsessed by the idea that if you had to live at all you might as well live where the weather was warm. But where to go? And until the house was sold, what to go on? Between the hospital and the traveling expenses, Aunt Anna's bequest was nearly gone.

As events began to transpire, they indicated that Mother, on the other side of the veil, was starting to put pressure on my life. I was being invisibly guided, even though at the time I would never have believed it. Just when I was most discouraged, a letter came from Salt Lake City, which had always seemed like paradise lost to me ever since it had been one of our unachieved goals in my childhood. The letter was from my friend Margaret Sanders, who had gone there to study sculpture at the University of Utah. Margaret is the daughter of Colonel Harlan Sanders, who was later to become famous as the Kentucky Fried Chicken colossus. At that time he was just getting it under way, having opened his first franchised restaurant in Salt Lake City.

"It's Heaven on Earth here," Margaret wrote, bombarding me with descriptions of the ideal climate.

So why not? I started making immediate plans. Nina debated whether to take an apartment alone in Oakland, or come with me. I would have loved to have her along, being entirely fed up with traveling by myself to strange places and also being very fond of Nina. But I wouldn't urge her. She had to make her own decision. She didn't want to leave Oakland and her music pupils, but neither did she want me to go traipsing off again without her.

"I'll go for the life of adventure," she finally announced; we agreed to point ourselves westward once more, this time together.

Once our thoughts were focused, events took shape rapidly. The price of the house was reduced for quick sale; it was claimed in a week. Two weeks later we had an auction of all our household goods, packed the car, stored some things, and were all ready to leave.

Who said pioneering days were over? There she was, a little seventy-two-year-old woman, small and frail but valiantly leaving the town and the friends she'd grown to love, just to accompany me because I had a roving urge. That was a little pioneering woman. So off we started on a cold, rainy morning in late September—Nina, Susy and Junior heading into the unknown once again. This time it was to bring rewards undreamed of.

NINE

WHICH SPOON TO STIR THE GRAVY?

Driving along toward Salt Lake City, the car piled awkwardly with all our belongings, I told Nina, "Life would be so much simpler for us if we lived in a trailer."

She squeaked with alarm.

"We could take our home with us like a turtle," I went on, the possibilities appealing to me more and more.

My companion didn't like the idea at all. "If you get one, I'm not traveling with you," she said, more prophetic than she knew.

When we arrived in Salt Lake City, I did buy a twenty-two foot house trailer, though, just barely the right size for the two of us. It was cozy and cute and we enjoyed squeezing into it. We parked it and called it the Gingerbread House.

I was soon doing *Shopping with Susy* columns for the *Salt Lake Tribune* and the *Deseret News* and a full tabloid page in the Sunday *Tribune*. This involved going to stores with a large Polaroid camera and taking pictures of the objects I was to describe in the paper. It wasn't the right kind of camera for the work, and stooping and squatting in the store aisles without proper lighting was very difficult. Eventually the paper hired a photographer with proper camera and lighting equipment to accompany me on my rounds. All went smoothly after that.

I've often been puzzled about why I've so continually gotten into situations where it seemed necessary to overcome some complex obstacle without the proper training. Why was it unavoidable that I spend weeks trying to broadcast with tapes made on the wrong kind of recorder when *Shopping with Susy* was on the air? Why did I have to run a complicated newspaper typing machine without anyone around to give instructions? Why did I try to teach myself professional photography with a camera unequipped for the work?

Sure, I got into those things because of my ignorance and stayed with them because of my persistence, but they always seemed inevitable and I never knew how to get out of them without giving up and admitting defeat, which I was too stubborn to do.

Now I'm thankful for this training in perseverance and in enduring stressful situations. Because of it, I was able to struggle with the difficulties I later encountered with "the other side" and not break under the strain. I had acquired the determination to overcome whatever problems presented themselves, no matter how confusing they became. It prepared me well.

Among the new friends I made in Salt Lake City was Veryl Smith, who frequently improved the shining morning hours with me over a cup of coffee. One night in January she told Nina and me, while having dinner with us in the Gingerbread House, that she'd met a girl who had a Ouija board and said she got frequent messages from the spirit world. Veryl's big gray eyes were bright with anticipation as she said, "I told her to bring her board to my house tomorrow night and we'd give it a try."

"You can't be serious," I laughed. "Why that's just a child's toy. Or, if you take it seriously, it's black magic, strictly from the Dark Ages."

Nina wasn't amused. She was afraid for Veryl. "You don't know what you're letting yourself in for," she said gravely. Then she told us that she had known a spirit medium long ago, a Mrs. Perkins of Indianapolis, who had achieved amazing results communicating with other realms but had become unsettled in the process.

"I'm afraid you'll run into things you can't handle," Nina warned Veryl.

When my friend phoned a few days later, she had nothing to relate. They hadn't entertained any unseen personages after all.

"No luck. Nobody came to our party," Veryl told us. Nina was relieved.

Several weeks later I saw *The Unobstructed Universe* by Stewart Edward White on the bookshelf of an acquaintance who was entertaining us at dinner, and exclaimed, "Why, we had this at home." A relative of Nina's had sent it to us long ago, but not one of us had ever read it. I'd given it to the library along with most of our other books when we left Oakland.

"What's it about?" I asked.

"I haven't read it," its owner said, "but it's supposed to try to show that people continue to live after death."

I glanced through it, picking up in passing terms like "receptivity" and "conductivity" and "impetus" and others that meant nothing to me in the context in which they were being used.

"How obtuse can you get?" I wondered, but still there was a compulsion to read it. I borrowed it. Nina and Veryl were also interested, so the next night we sat down to peruse it aloud together and discuss it.

The book is supposed to be a true account of messages obtained, through a nonprofessional medium, from White's wife, Betty, who had died some months before. This well known author, a man of obvious personal integrity, related several instances where he received information that he was convinced could have come from no one but his dead wife, and even to us skeptical readers it sounded so authentic it made our spines tingle.

White's wife Betty is the one who made the statement quoted earlier, "Consciousness is the only reality and consciousness is in a state of evolution." This didn't mean much to us in those days before the physicists began talking about it. Now we have such statements as this from Rupert Sheldrake, eminent Cambridge biologist, who speaks of "a creative consciousness which transcends the universe, and that is the source of its existence and of the laws that govern it." And Gary and Linda's book *The Living Energy Universe*, published in October, 1999, gives information that leads them to say: "Wouldn't it be wonderful if our loved ones, as expressed in their info-energy systems, maintained their integrity and identity as they extended into space and became an integral part of the fabric of eternal light? Like the light of distant stars, their 'dissolving' souls were still unique and whole, entangled with us dynamically and eternally? This is a sweet vision indeed."

Another good quote comes from my friend Mary Schneider, who has a great unpublished manuscript called *Parvati:* "Consciousness pervades everything through and through. It is consciousness itself that pretends to divide reality into mind and matter, bodies and souls. Whatever you perceive, whatever you experience is but the play of consciousness and therefore transitory. And, in its time, every perceivable thing within this sea of ceaseless change will perish like a dream; consciousness alone remains, forever present." But here I am quoting present-day authors, yet my narrative is still back in 1955 when I was getting this basic information from Stewart Edward White and was soon to have it confirmed from the spirit world by William James.

Because of its unusual terminology, a lot of *The Unobstructed Universe* was difficult for me to read, but James later gave me almost the same information in simpler words. Among other things, James explained:

> The first phase of life after death has been adequately described as "unobstructed" in comparison

with the Earth plane which is "obstructed" by matter, for we exist in dimensions of space and time at variance with your own. To your senses, matter is solid. To a spirit, matter is not solid. It is no obstruction to him; he can pass right through it. Even time as you know it on Earth is not an obstruction to us because we are in no way dependent on time—there is no day or night for us. If we wish to travel, we think ourselves where we want to be and we are there, so distance is no obstruction to us either.

White calls the spirit body the "Beta" body, which appears to be just like the physical body. Because one looks and feels the same as he did while on Earth, the newly deceased is often unaware that any change has taken place. This confusion is compounded by finding himself in the same location, perhaps beside a bed in which there is a form that appears to be himself, but he's sure it cannot be because he feels so alive and well.

"There are always progressed entities who greet this new arrival in the spirit world and attempt to tell him the truth about his condition, if he will listen to them," James writes. "He is told that he has passed through the experience called death and that the power of his thought controls everything in the dimension where he now finds himself."

People who have just died learn that the spirit body is affected entirely by mind power, so they will look however they are used to thinking of themselves. At first, they appear exactly as they did when they died, no matter how miserable and decrepit they may have been. But as soon as they learn how to control their thoughts and begin their character development, they change in appearance, for the improvement is reflected in their looks. Spirits who have begun to progress are beautiful, for they have learned to think of themselves as they were during the period of their greatest physical fitness and happiness on Earth. Those who died with wickedness in their hearts were probably rather sinister-looking and they will remain that way until their thoughts about themselves change. This assuredly won't occur until they begin to improve their character.

When you go over, how you look is comparable to how you act. To get off to a good start, therefore, you should die aware of your need for self-improvement. If you do, according to my correspondent:

> Life after death is so challenging and so marvelously engrossing that life on Earth is nothing in comparison. I can truthfully say that when you come to this sphere you will find so much to interest and excite you that I cannot make it sound attractive enough. But you have to keep your mind open when you arrive in order to get started off properly and save yourself much wasted time, just as you have to keep your mind alert to new ideas and new opportunities on Earth. The person with a closed mind, who will not allow any new concepts to enter his philosophy, will have an even duller time after death than he did on Earth. He will have it, that is, until he wakes up and starts his progression. Advancement is inevitable. No consciousness which ever inhabited the body of a man on Earth or any other inhabited planet is ever lost forever. All must ultimately reach the heights of achievement. The fact that they have to work to do it is what discourages some of them from starting, and what encourages others that it will be a challenge.

To me these ideas, which I first met in White's book, were new and strange, but interesting. I didn't want to be charged with having a closed mind, yet all this seemed awfully far-fetched—yet intriguing. Definitely intriguing.

Nina was never one to argue about her beliefs, but she had accepted the idea of after-death survival long ago and saw what we were coming across in our reading as just an amplification of what she already knew in Christianity.

Veryl was as interested as I, though not inclined to argue with the material as much. She and Nina were in sympathy with my efforts to assimilate it, for when we finished *The Unobstructed Universe*, I kept mulling it over. It presented a concept more inviting than any I'd encountered before, and it wouldn't let me alone. It teased me and titillated my thinking. Soon I succumbed to the interest it aroused. I went to the library and got another book by White, called *With Folded Wings*.

As we read it aloud together one Sunday afternoon, we came upon the statement that our loved ones who have passed on would like to communicate with us to reassure us there is no death and that they are often with us. White said that if we will make the first move toward contact, they'll cooperate.

The idea of communication, the way White told it, was plausible enough if there really were spirits around. If, as he insisted, our friends are still hovering about, why shouldn't they want us to know it, to relieve our grieving for them if that was the case, to assuage their egos, for that matter—for who would want to be totally ignored all the time? Also, when they became aware of one who was in terror of the gaping void of death, wouldn't they feel an intense desire to say, "Look, it isn't like that at all. I'm still here; you'll be here. There's more to all this than meets the eye."

As a theory it sounded all right, but I didn't buy it. Still, the chance that it might be possible was enthralling. I stopped reading and went outside for a walk with Junior to consider whether or not, in all seriousness, I ought to try to reach my parents, to prove to myself the truth or fallacy of all this.

Suddenly, on that crisp, sunny afternoon in March, as my dog and I ambled through a large field covered with dried grass and weeds, I was infused with awareness of Mother's warm, loving presence. She was so real and so *there* that I almost felt as if she was giving me one of her big bear hugs.

This was an incredible thing to me, coming just when it did, for I'd never had such a feeling of her closeness in all the six years since Mother's death. Life took on an immediate new dimension, which I knew it would never lose. It was a beautifully tender confirmation of the hope for survival. No matter what happened to me in the future, I would always cherish this experience and be eager to recapture it.

I said aloud, "Mother, if it's possible that you might still be alive somewhere, I'm going to spend the rest of my life trying to prove it."

So that is how it all began. I have since learned that thousands upon thousands of people have felt the presence of loved ones who have died. But besides cherishing this experience, I have done something about it. For the past forty-nine years, I have been critically investigating every aspect of the supernatural. I've argued the pros and cons of the possibility of spirit survival. I've developed an apparently successful mode of communication. And as you will see when I have detailed my adventures, it has ultimately resulted in the preparation of a website where individuals can register to leave codes they can try to break after their deaths.

TEN

WE TRY THE OUIJA

The morning after my sensational experience, I awoke sensible and material-minded again. When the memory of that feeling of Mother's presence began to warm me, I stopped myself short with: "Let's be rational about this. It must have been a sensory illusion."

I knew that the subconscious mind can play strange tricks. Heavens, I'd read enough about analysis at college. I'd had a go at deciphering Freud, Jung and Adler. I knew about self-suggestion and what it could do.

"But this wasn't something from inside. Mother was actually there. It couldn't be anything else but that," I argued with myself.

According to psychologists, the subconscious mind is capable of producing many unusual experiences if one secretly desires them. Wasn't this more likely an unsuspected urge to escape back into the womb? Was I running once again to Mother for protection from the big bad world?

If this had started happening to me at almost any other time of my life, that surely could have been the explanation. If it had occurred during my lonely stay in the desert, it would have been obvious that I was reaching out for security. But now I had Nina, Margaret and her twelve-year-old son Trigg for constant companionship. With a cozy home, an interesting job and an active social life, I was stable and settled enough that there were no big emotional problems of any sort confronting me. I was even enjoying better physical health than ever before.

Well, if this were Mother, the smartest thing she'd done was to wait to try to get in touch with me until I was ready for it.

For days I went round and round like this. I'd start to glow with the remembrance of that moment of illumination, then I'd reject it and get on with washing my hair, or writing an ad for a lamp, or walking Junior or whatever the project at hand might be. If I had just let it go at that, the experience would soon have receded to a pleasant memory of an unusual moment in my life and that would have been the end of it.

But that damned curiosity of mine wouldn't let it lay. Finally I told Veryl to borrow the Ouija and we'd have a go at it, and with that step I opened my own personal Pandora's box, letting myself in for the most hazardous adventures of my life.

We were leery of using a mere toy, but there wasn't any other way we knew to try communication. The Ouija board is supposed to be the nearest thing to a telegraph-between-worlds, and we thought it was the only way for beginners to make contact. It's certainly a most unprepossessing instrument for a serious investigation, being a board which has the letters of the alphabet and the numbers from one to ten on it, and a little plastic heart-shaped pointer (called a planchette), about the size of your hand with tiny short legs like Junior's. Two people put the board on their knees and one hand each on the pointer. Then, if you're lucky, it moves around on top of the board and indicates certain letters. If you're even luckier, they spell words that make sense and sometimes give intelligent messages.

The only thing one can be sure of about a Ouija board is this: when *seriously* attempting to communicate, those who have their fingers on the pointer do not deliberately push the planchette around and direct it to the different letters. It moves by some force that does not come consciously from the people involved. Thus when sensible answers to questions are written, it is a very eerie business indeed.

Spirit communicators such as James and Mother advise me to warn people away from Ouijas and automatic writing until they have learned how to be fully protected. They say that innocent efforts at communication are as dangerous as playing with matches or hand grenades. They have me as Exhibit A of what not to do, for I experienced many of the worst problems of such involvement. Had I been forewarned that such efforts run the risk of causing mental disturbance, I might have been more wary. That is one reason I continue to make my adventures public, to prevent others from getting into situations which might prove even more damaging to them than they did to me. In later years, Veryl Smith knew a woman who got so involved with the Ouija and the romancing of her alleged spirit lover that she killed herself to be with him.

But Veryl and I, not knowing what a gamble it was, were determined to proceed, and since we had nothing else available, we used the Ouija to begin our scientific safari. It was certainly a most unorthodox expedition into research, as Veryl and Susy, with board on knees and planchette under fingers, crossed over into the unknown and moved out into uncharged territory, alone and unguided.

We sat there for about ten minutes. Nothing happened, except that I got a kink in my back. Lacking the fortitude of the intrepid explorer, I said, "To hell with it" and went into the trailer's bedroom to lie down and recuperate.

Veryl, still with the board on her knees and her fingers resting idly on the pointer, suggested, "Call your mother. Maybe that will set the force in motion."

So I entreated, "Mother, if it's possible, please talk to us."

"Susy, come here quick!" cried Veryl, for just as my words had been spoken she had felt a sudden surge through her arm and the planchette had jumped under her hand.

I hurried back and sat down again. As soon as my fingers touched the planchette, it spelled: "It is Mother. I . . . love . . . you . . . I love you." Then in answer to our questions, with frequent incoherences as if Mother were having difficulty making the apparatus work for her, it spelled her full name, my father's name and the date of Mother's birthday. It was interesting, but there was no way to be sure it was Mother. I could have been feeding it unconsciously all the data reported. When we asked about Veryl's family, the answers were also correct, but Veryl knew them. Although positive we weren't consciously pushing it, we were not sure about anything else. Where those words were coming from was a mystery.

To test the material, we would have to ask questions to which neither of us knew the answers—but how could we then be sure the reply was right? We decided to ask the name of a neighbor's mother, and when told "Elsie," I ran over to check with him. He said "No." We tried for half an hour more, and a series of names was trotted out that would have entranced any old time Mormon husband. We received Josephine, Amanda, Sylvia, Kate, Martha, Adelaide, Genevieve, Brunhilda, Matilda . . . and each time our neighbor, who was sticking his head in the trailer window by now to see what was going on, snickered and shook his head.

To this day we don't know what his mother's name was. He never enlightened us, and twitted us about it whenever we saw him after that, for he was sure we'd been taken in by our own subconscious minds. By then we were sure, too. It would have taken no end of argument to convince me that Mother had had anything to do with the proceedings. All those names didn't sound like anything she would fool around with, and I didn't know then that other spirits might try to use the Ouija board without being personally invited.

Yet if there were even one chance in a trillion—let's not be small about this, one in a quintillion—that it was Mother, I was going to make every effort to find out. If my mother (or anyone else, for that matter) was trying to prove to me that there is no death, I wouldn't let her down in that endeavor.

A few nights later we tried again, without making any effort to test our source, but with a serious objective to our questioning nonetheless. What we were actually doing was trying to salve our consciences. Since our last session, we had read somewhere that spirits were able to know what was in people's minds, so we were feeling uneasy. If there was a chance that I was going to be holding mental open house for Mother, I'd best do a bit of spring cleaning first.

Our initial question after the pointer wrote "Betty Smith is here" was "Do you know about the secret things that go on among Earth people?"

The answer came: "We are so far above it that it doesn't matter." (The communicants later explained that advanced spirits invariably have the good taste not to intrude into our most private thoughts or intimate moments unless they have been especially requested to.) At that we gave sighs of relief. Then we asked, "Can you read our minds?"

"Yes."

Blushing a little I said, "When people do things that you used to think were bad when you were on Earth, do you now understand why they do them?"

"Yes."

"Am I forgiven?"

"Kiss."

I took that kindly. Up until the last remark I had been entirely suspicious that it was my own subconscious mind doing it. But that word "Kiss" sounded just like Mother and not at all like me talking to myself.

We didn't tire of this new amusement, and on the night of April 16, Veryl, Nina, and I took turns playing with it (Nina seemed to have become reconciled that we weren't taking our efforts seriously enough to endanger ourselves).

After a few exchanges that purported to come from Mother, we began to receive messages from Nina's mother, whose first name was Kizzie.

"Nina is not going to 'love' long," the Ouija wrote. "Nina won't love long."

Both Veryl and I began talking at once about what a "silly" message it was. Nina was so sleepy she hadn't noticed the strange wording, but in a little over a month the message would come true.

ELEVEN

PENCILS START WRITING

"Get a pencil." That was the instruction my Ouija board gave me one day after we'd been operating it at a loss for several weeks. This is the traditional invitation to do automatic writing. I asked how to go about receiving messages with a pencil, and the Ouija answered, "Go into a trance." Now how did one do that? I thought you had to be a born medium to accomplish trance, or else be mesmerized by a gentleman with piercing black eyes and hocus-pocus hands.

Naturally I gave it a whirl. I went into my bedroom, closed the door and lay on the bed in the dark, a pencil in my hand and a large pad of paper under it.

"Go ahead, entrance me," I said. Nothing happened. I tried to make my mind a blank and stayed quiet, hoping for the best. Still nothing happened.

Nina kept calling to me, "Are you all right? Are you sure you're all right?" She was pacing the trailer floor—two steps north and then two steps south—nearly frantic for fear I'd strip my gears, knock myself out, swallow my tongue or start having convulsions. For nearly an hour I drew a complete blank. I couldn't go into a trance at all. In fact, I have never been able to go at will into a decent trance. I am also impossible to hypnotize. I'm one of those obstinate persons who resists even when trying hardest to be accommodating and to get the "thinker" out of the way.

So I just lay there, hoping good intentions and complete relaxation were the next best substitute. Finally, after a long time, a message began to write itself on the paper. It was the most peculiar feeling I'd ever experienced. The hand was just writing by itself without my conscious will being involved in any way. It wrote scragglingly across the page in run-together words, "I am your Mother and I love you. There is lots to tell you but it is hard to do. Love to Nina. I'll write more next time. Betty."

I came out of the bedroom floating on my own personal warm, fuzzy cloud. Imagine receiving a letter from your mother who's been dead six years! It was hardly likely. It didn't make sense. But there it was in black and white, written by hand on paper right before my eyes. It was tremendously exhilarating.

As time passed, the elation simmered down into debates with myself about what had really occurred, for with every new day came a new argument as to whether it actually had been Mother writing or my subconscious mind playing potsy with me. Nonetheless, I continued trying to maintain the correspondence.

Each night after dinner I'd settle down with pencil and paper for a chat. Soon the writing would come just as well with my eyes open, sitting at the table in the little living-dining area. My communicant and I practiced and found that we wrote best when all the words were attached to each other, as she had originally done it. But, oh, the problems of deciphering the script afterward, when we typed up each evening's efforts!

Most of our first sessions were spent practicing control, and we did rows of circles and up-and-down strokes, which only too vividly recalled my childhood days of penmanship classes so boringly endured.

Just the fact of sitting there accomplishing nothing more than circles, when I was so eager to receive evidence, inclined me to believe that it wasn't initiated within my own mind, and when the messages did finally start, they seemed of so little import they just couldn't have come from me. My sublime subliminal surely would have produced more interesting palaver than "Love is the most important thing. You must learn to love your fellow men."

Most of the time it was drudgery to sit and try to blank my mind so as to be receptive. After the thrill of receiving the first letter from Mother had subsided, it was never again an emotional experience for me. I felt no urge to write, just the desire to be successful in this new endeavor. My stubbornness, as of yore, kept me at it—that and the bare possibility that it actually might be Mother. I never experience, as some people do who receive automatic writing, a sudden impulse to grab the pencil, or any other indication that the force, external or internal, is eager to write. Sometimes when a percipient or agent or medium, whatever you want to call it, is in a valid trancelike state, unknown foreign languages are received, or the script may come upside down or backwards. Even mirror writing, which can only be read when held up to a looking glass, has come on many occasions, but these sorts of things usually occur only to powerful psychics. This never has happened to me because I have never been able to withdraw my conscious awareness from what is going on. This made me almost sure it *was* all originating in the dark jungles of my nether mind. My own thoughts and beliefs were sometimes evident in the writing, for my mind was right there personally running things even when I was trying hardest to blank myself out of controlling it. This, I learned from Stewart Edward White, is called "coloring."

A medium or psychic—a person who is more receptive or sensitive than others to impressions from the spirit world—is not a machine. No matter how withdrawn into trance one may be, there is still one's own mind to contend with, to a greater or lesser extent depending upon the amount of withdrawal and the psychic power available. So there is the possibility of the medium's own mental participation altering, in terms of personal experience or understanding, the message coming through. *Coloring.* It's as if the telegraph instrument kept trying to get into the act with its own interpretation of the transmitted dispatch

Here was I, no medium at all, and never anything but completely conscious when doing automatic writing. Naturally I intruded, and no wonder so few evidential messages came. After more than forty years, it still surprises me when I receive material I have no way of knowing or conjecturing—but my communicants have occasionally startled me with genuine evidence.

After reading about this perplexity called coloring, I would ask Mother if what she had just written had been colored. If it was mixed up, or not quite clear, she would usually say it had been. Then she would try again, and she managed to get it straight after a second or third attempt.

Often, I consciously anticipated the next word to be written, but if it was not what Mother intended she crossed it out and persisted until she finally wrote what she wanted. She was just as insistent upon getting her thoughts through without distortion as I was in unwittingly interfering, and we fought it out until our battles themselves were an indication to me that it *must* be an outside force. I mean, if there were that much inner conflict, wouldn't it be evident to others that I was ready for the funny farm?

The fight she was having with my coloring and questioning and doubting gave my communicant a rough time, too. It's no wonder her messages were for the most part routine, but I was always disappointed when our hour's work produced only dissertations on such topics as "loving your fellow man" and "development of character" and "positive thinking." I could have written essays on them myself, without going to all the trouble of automatic writing. It was boring to accomplish what seemed to be so little. Yet Mother gradually made her point, by dint of sheer repetition, that I personally must adopt the ethics she was insisting upon.

is the most important thing and you need to love ," she wrote. "You must learn to think more kindly ou are much too critical. You need to love every- y those to whom you are attached and who are kind to you. It takes real work to love everyone, do it. And then everything will go smoothly an happy all the time."

I began to make a special effort to try this as never before. When it was difficult, Mother gave me pep talks, at times when it wasn't expected at all. For instance, when asked if she had any message for me one night, she answered: "I want to tell you to love, love, love everyone all the time. You need to love more than you do. Love everyone every minute and your life will be a big success while you are on Earth as well as afterwards. Heaven is the state of love."

Mother seemed to feel that compassion, understanding and sympathy were fairly good counterparts for this love that is so difficult to attain; and I must go on record as saying that she was right. Even the consistent effort to have compassion and understanding for others makes an immediate change in your life. This soon became evident in mine, and then I was glad she'd been so determined about it.

One thing Mother wrote that wasn't hard to accept was that at the time of her death, when she had said, "I wish someone would tell me where I am," it was because she had suddenly seen Daddy and Aunt Ivy. And she'd said, "Don't leave me" to *them*.

I was told that since his death in 1933, my father had concentrated on his spiritual advancement. After he'd seen to it that Mother was properly oriented in her new environment and was keeping an eye on me, he went ahead to another dimension to continue his progression.

James has since assured me time and time again that every aspect of the work they undertake to improve themselves and begin their progression is interesting and challenging. This is most reassuring. I was always suspicious of a Heaven in which there is no work. Having responsibilities to meet and tasks that must be accomplished is essential to peace of mind, so it's encouraging to learn that constructive effort that is not drudgery still goes on after death.

"Nothing here need seem dull or routine," James says, "for what you are doing can almost always be made pleasurable. When you have achieved the highest point of development one is capable of attaining in the etheric plane, you pass on to more advanced dimensions farther away from Earth. Life on the higher spirit planes of existence becomes unbelievably happy at all times."

Margaret Sanders, who is an excellent sculptress, spent most of her time in Salt Lake City doing huge clay portraits. But she was curious about what I was up to and interested in hearing about it. Once, while writing automatically in her presence, I handed the pencil to her and it kept right on going, with an answer to a question for her.

"That's spooky!" she cried, quickly giving the pencil back to me. Then she understood that I was not consciously pushing it myself. It seemed to me that she watched my undertaking with more interest after that.

As time went on, I was never to receive any one big piece of evidence, and yet the many small inexplicable incidents added up to something highly curious. For those who are chomping at the bit waiting for exciting scientific proof to be revealed in this book—it will never come. However, the sheer number of minor incidents carefully observed and recorded amount to some reassuring indications that I have been in touch with surviving entities. And the delineation of their personalities, particularly Mother's, comes to have significance as time goes on.

As my guardian angel, Mother revealed her sweet but bossy self in many ways. When she told me she was playing this role in my life, I asked her, "How can we develop our own character if we are constantly guarded and guided by someone invisible?"

Mother replied that guardian angels can give suggestions and warnings that may be extremely helpful to us on occasion, but they do not want to tell us what to do with our lives, for it is by making our own decisions that we grow. Mother tried to maintain this attitude, but she was still human enough and *herself* enough not always to be able to manage it. She sometimes still told me "what spoon to stir the gravy with." It was natural that she would do what she could to make life easier for me, however, and it was very pleasing to think that someone might be handy to make an occasional effort on my behalf.

One of these efforts was when we made a dress together. Early in May I decided to see if Mother could help me sew, and she said she'd give it a whirl. If it worked, it would be a feather in her (etheric) cap, for I had never been able to use a sewing machine comfortably or successfully in my life. Its sounds and movements made me nervous. I do everything backward and grumble and cuss and hate it. But Mother said if I would just remain passive and let her do the thinking, she might be able to help.

Somebody should have been thinking when the material was purchased, for I came home with fabric whose stripes were designed to go horizontally and a pattern to make them vertically. When the pattern was spread out on the table, the instructions overwhelmed me and I became agitated as usual. I could no more have relaxed and let Mother take over than I could have roped a cow.

Within moments there was a knock at the door and Loraine, a young woman who lived in the trailer on our left, came in. She so seldom visited us that she was as surprised as we were that she'd gotten a sudden notion to show us her new hairdo. Then she asked, "What are you doing?"

"Trying to cut out a dress, but I haven't the foggiest idea how to do it."

"Let me help you," Loraine said. "I've made my own clothes since I was a child." She not only cut the dress out but explained what must be done. Then she brought over her own sewing machine so we wouldn't have to rent one.

After Loraine left at about eleven o'clock, I took pencil in hand to tell Mother what had happened. She was way ahead of me, replying that she hadn't been up to teaching me at this late date how to cut out a pattern when she'd had such poor luck with it in bygone years.

"I put the idea into Loraine's mind to come over so that she could help you," she wrote.

It had to be coincidence. I couldn't accept it as anything else, no matter what the pencil wrote. But how to account for the fact that when my sewing started the next day, I was almost an expert? I never once seamed the wrong sides of the material together, as invariably used to happen. I was able to work out problems of facings, buttonholes, plackets, zippers—things that previously had eluded me. And I was as calm and happy as Mother would have been—as she always was at home, her old sewing machine humming.

The dress came out fine, so I rushed out and bought more material and made a skirt for Nina and another dress and a sunsuit for myself before the joint endeavor ended.

This sewing experience persuaded Nina that Mother really *was* making her presence felt, and from then on she never had any doubts about our communication.

It was persuasive for me, too, especially because I have never since been able to achieve that kind of rapport with Mother when sewing and so have reverted to my previous ineptitude.

At the time, though, I had high hopes that we would maintain the closeness all the time. I decided that sewing was just the thing to while away spare hours, with Mother at the throttle doing the mental work while I, you might say, just lent a hand and a knee to the proceedings.

TWELVE

A PREDICTION COMES TRUE—
NINA DOESN'T "LOVE" LONG

My absorption in the adventure of communicating was complete. Still, I worked at my job every day, competently enough, no doubt, and no one suspected that my main interest lay in our evening séances, when I took pencil in hand and tried to prove to myself that there is no death.

While at first it had been more of a fun thing, it developed for a brief period in May into a very trying situation. This centered around the manuscript of the book about my Florida experiences, which I had started in the desert and completed in Maryland. Although sensing that it was a feeble effort, I thought that perhaps it was worth sending to a publisher and had mailed it off in March. It could be expected to take as long as three months before an answer might come, either accepting or rejecting it, so I put it out of my mind most of the time.

One evening in late May when doing automatic writing I asked, "Mother, tell me what is going on with my book. Do they like it?" The reply was that the publisher adored it and would let me know it soon. While somewhat encouraged, I was too wary to accept this as convincing, and dropped the matter. But the communications wouldn't let it go. Even when I had no intention of asking about it, preferring—or at least thinking it more advisable—to write about impersonal things, the subject was brought up every night. The book would be published very soon, it was said. Word about it was coming within the next few weeks. I'd be flying to New York in early June.

A novice who sends out a first manuscript is, of course, more anxious and apprehensive about it than is a seasoned author. Still, I would have spent little time worrying about the reception of this manuscript, except that I was made unnecessarily concerned with it because of the constant talk about it, and was not able to completely convince myself that it wasn't information from Mother.

Finally one night, after another attempt to get an evidential message from Mother so that I could make sure I was genuinely in touch with her and that the information concerning my manuscript wasn't just the result of my own desire, I tried a test that was provable, asking if Margaret had gotten a job she was applying for that day. The reply was Yes, she would go to work Monday. I was even told her salary. So I phoned her and said, "Congratulations on your new job."

"I didn't get it," she said. "It was filled before I got there."

I was intensely chagrined, almost agonized. Mother couldn't have lied to me, so evidently the whole communication process had just been a figment of my own fancy. I'd been making a fool of myself for many weeks.

"Either Mother has been writing, or I'm sick," I cried to Nina in despair.

"Honey, I know you've been writing to your mother at least part of the time," she consoled me. Then she offered an idea that had never occurred to me. "Maybe another spirit writes sometimes and claims to be Betty."

"Do you really suppose it could be that?" I asked. "Wouldn't that be against the rules?"

Somewhat cheered, however, by that possibility, I took up the pencil again, this time making a point to ask for identification. When the pencil started moving of its own accord, I asked, "Who is writing?"

"Your mother."

"What's your name?"

"Betty Smith."

"Your full name?"

"Elizabeth Maude Anderson Hardegen Smith."

"What was the name of our first dog?"

"Arapaho Mountain Lassie."

This data was correct, so I took a chance and went ahead with the writing, insisting on being told what was going on. Mother said the misinformation had been written by spirit intruders, who were sometimes able to exert more power than she and so could push her aside and gain control of my pencil. She said that she had tried constantly to warn me about them on the few occasions lately when she had been my communicant, but that the awareness of their activity wasn't in my mind, and she couldn't put it there. She cautioned me always to test with personal questions before accepting anything further as coming from her.

"Then I guess all this business about my book came from them," I said, and Mother agreed. She added, however, that a letter from the publisher was actually in the mail for me at that moment and that I would receive it the next day. When I asked her whether or not it would be favorable, she said my mind was so preoccupied with the subject that she would be unable to get the truth through to me. She warned against ever trying to query her about things I was too closely involved with, because my own coloring would change the message. This is true of all mediums, I have learned. They know better than to count on personal information they receive.

Still, Mother had given me a specific date when I would hear from the publisher. This was the first time anything of such a definite nature had been received, so it put her on the spot. As I waited with jitters for the mail to come the next day, I realized that my belief in the veracity of the communications hinged on whether or not the letter was forthcoming.

It was! The publisher didn't want my book, but I wasn't downhearted, because Mother had passed her first test, and that cheered me up. It was exasperating that those interloping ghouls had gotten me so stirred up over it, though.

I began to check back over all my automatic writing and understand that much of the time, when I had blamed my coloring or my subconscious for inconsistencies, they could have been caused by intruders. Apparently, unenlightened spirits delight in interrupting efforts at communication, just for the pleasure of making their presence known to someone on Earth. They will write any kind of gibberish; it doesn't matter to them what is said. They might even deliberately try to cause confusion. Invisible pranksters can be very naughty if they wish. I was struck then with the realization that often I'd been specter-hectored during the past months.

James later explained how people can act so unpleasantly after they become spirits. Maybe they were unpleasant in various other ways before they died:

> There is no precipitate transition from living on Earth to living in the next dimension. If an individual is prepared for this fact—that the adaptation to the life of spirit is a gradual one—he is better able to accept it when it happens to him. We have always thought that if we lived at all after death we would have to be entirely transformed immediately into something ethereal. We expect, if we expect anything at all, a change of conditions so vast as to put us into an altogether different state. When this does not occur, we are confused and find it difficult to accept. But I must make it clear that your transition is gradual for a very definite reason. Supreme Intelligence planned it that way as the most sensible and workable arrangement for man's progression.

You see, at your death you are the same you, and nobody else. You are the person you were, with the same characteristics, the same attitudes, thoughts, memories, likes, dislikes and habits. You have now left a physical body that is no longer of use to you, and you are going to have to learn how to get along without it. Therefore, James says, in order for you not to find this so overpoweringly confusing that you are unable to cope, you are permitted by the system to live in your spiritual body in such close proximity to Earth that you can continue to feel at home in your new environment. James continued:

> It must be noted that you are on your own after death just as much as you are during your lifetime on Earth. There are those who will make every effort to help you and to tell you the truth. You are informed by them that you are a spiritual being who will live forever and that you must now bend your efforts toward progressing to a state of perfection; you are given to understand, however, that you can make your progress at your own rate of speed and that you do not have to leave the Earth environment until you are thoroughly ready.
>
> Until you listen to all this you will make mistakes, just as you do now. You do not arrive at the feet of St. Peter or anyone else who will judge you, direct you, and make everything all right for you. You have, instead, to choose your own paths and make your decisions just as you always did. You have the help of teachers and guides who can give you assistance if you will take it; but you are no more likely to listen to them after your death than you were to listen to advice on Earth. If you were a warm, loving, open-minded person, you will probably have relatives of a similar nature to greet you and you will heed them. But if you were the kind of an individual who never could be told anything, you will still be that kind of person. If you knew all the answers on Earth, you will think you do in the next life, and will continue to act the same as you always did until you

finally begin to realize that you are getting nowhere. Then out of pure boredom or misery you will pay attention to those who state the facts to you.

Intruding spirits are called "Earthbound," being so attached to the physical aspects of life or to the sorrows or sensations to which they were accustomed that they continue to cling to them. Drug addicts and alcoholics are particularly Earthbound, remaining close to those like themselves on Earth in an effort to continue getting their kicks, if only vicariously, James said. Then he went on:

There is nothing that keeps all these unhappy souls in that disagreeable condition, except their lack of a desire to improve themselves, or their inability to accept elucidating truths. It may take some of them, who have led dissolute or criminal lives, many hundreds of years before they face up to the fact that they must work on themselves in order to leave the unpleasantness in which they find themselves. When they do start to make an effort, it is very difficult for them because it is work on their character development and their thinking techniques, and they have little or no character and their thinking is about as negative as it is possible to be. If they had been aware of this in time and labored for improvement on Earth, they would not now find themselves in such miserable circumstances.

Well, you wouldn't expect it to be as easy on those who had been rotten on Earth as on those who had at least tried to live worthwhile existences. It was appalling to me to learn that these Earthbound types are the main ones who hang so closely around us and attempt to make their presence known whenever they find an opportunity. Someone working a Ouija board or doing automatic writing is someone opening his mental doors and crying out gaily to them, "Come in! Come in! Whoever you are!"

"Yes," agreed James, "they are particularly apt to intrude their presence on anyone who is attempting spirit communication of any sort. Some do it out of mischievousness, some out of genuine malevolence."

When I try to envision the type of spirit who would intrude himself upon those who cannot see him and attempt to disturb them mentally, or merely to josh them, I am naturally reminded of the nasty individual who spends his time calling people on the telephone and whispering filth into their ears before they can hang up. If such people weren't fortunate enough to be reclaimed into a decent person before death, they would be just the types who would reject assistance from well-meaning spirits after they died, continuing to ply their viciousness between planes of existence whenever they could. Someone communicating with spirits would be fair game for them.

Even though my efforts at writing during that first spring in Salt Lake City were not dependable, I didn't yet know the perils, so I wasn't about to stop trying to talk with Mother. I looked at it like this. Suppose you lived in a police state and every time you tried to get news from other countries over your radio, the government jammed the airwaves with static so that you got mostly garbled messages. Yet occasionally you received news so revealing about conditions on the other side of the boundary that you felt the urge to know more.

Suppose most people laughed at you and said, "Everyone knows there is nothing beyond," or, "It's illegal." Would you give up? Or would you continue trying, hoping to clarify your reception until you had something of definite value and positive proof to offer your fellow men?

But I didn't want to escape from reality, either, over this experience with the unknown, whether it was caused by conflict with my own subconscious or by spirit intruders. So, beginning to sense the very real dangers, I resolved to keep my feet on the ground ever firmer than before. I wrote very little after learning about Earthbound spirits and, always wary, asked for identification. Discovering that any hesitancy about the name of someone from my past indicated a trespasser, I'd stop the discourse immediately. It didn't take the phonies long to realize that it was no fun anymore working with a wise guy, and all but one of them went away.

This one usually identified himself. His name, he said, was Harvey, and he always got stuck trying to make the *H*, repeating the initial stroke several times. He didn't care what he said, he was just eager to write what he thought I wanted to hear. He particularly liked to write "I love you," for he presumed he could cajole me with that.

Harvey told me he was a carpenter who had died in Salt Lake City at the age of eighty. He said his last name was Boone, and at first, he was so horribly agreeable that he was perfectly willing to be Daniel's relative or any other Boone we suggested. In fact, he'd admit to being almost anyone—except the invisible rabbit named Harvey in the play and James Stewart movie of the same name. That he vehemently denied.

Harvey stuck to me like a Rocky Mountain spotted tick from the very first. Whenever I picked up the pencil in the loose way that indicated willingness to palaver for a while, no matter where I was—once even in a cocktail lounge—almost immediately it started to write, "I'm your Harvey. I'm here. I love you." When asked for Mother, he'd write, "I'm your mother" and if checks weren't made, he'd go on pretending. But he always flunked the personal questions and thus revealed himself. He heard me testing Mother with family names and learned enough of them that he could answer correctly, up to a point . . . until he gave himself away by the difficulty he had making his *H:* "What's your name?" "Betty Smith." "Your full name?" "Elizabeth Maude Anderson *H H H H H H.* . . . "

At first I believed Harvey to be harmless, but Mother kept telling me not to write with him or he'd hurt me. I couldn't figure out how he could hurt me, and besides, sometimes I was talking to him without being aware of it. How he harmed me, of course, was by keeping me from communicating with more enlightened spirits. If he said Mother wasn't around—"Not here, Mother's not here," he'd write—I'd believe him. Even though Mother insisted she would stay with me, I thought she must have been called away for a while on important business. Because if she was there, why did she let Harvey write? That business about him having more power than she did was pretty hard to take. Yet apparently it was true that when he flexed his mental muscles and exerted his strength, her force wasn't enough to overcome his.

Once someone suggested that Harvey might be a malefactor, so I asked him, "Are you a malefactor?"

"I don't know what that is," he wrote in reply.

"Are you harmful to me?"

"I don't want to hurt you," he answered. "I just want to stay with you. I love you." And stay he did, although the love he expressed was very selfish. He was obviously there only because he could talk to me.

Harvey became the butt of all our small jokes around the trailer—the little invisible man who hid things we misplaced, or who bumped our heads, or who got too much salt in our potatoes. And Margaret even blamed him for the chicken she lost to me on the Kentucky Derby.

She had been a longtime Lexington resident, so naturally she said, "Let's put a bet on the Derby" when we turned on the television to watch it.

"Who's running?" I asked her, not having paid enough attention to the race even to know the names of the horses.

She ticked them off on her fingers, "Well, there's Nashua, he's the favorite, and Summer Tan, and Swaps . . . "

"I'll take Swaps," I said, and we bet the chicken we were going to fry for dinner, Kentucky-style with the original herbs and spices, on the outcome. Swaps won. Wish that chicken had been a diamond ring.

Margaret said, "Harvey, that's no fair. You cheated, telling Susy."

So all right. Of course I don't think Harvey told me. There was no indication that he could predict the future anyway. Yet I had I never picked a winner before, at least not without studying such factors as who was the prettiest horse or which had the cutest jockey. Why would someone who has made a million wrong decisions start guessing right almost constantly when she begins dabbling with psychical phenomena? It was one of the first of the long string of more-than-coincidences that have occurred in my life since that April day when I first took the future in my hands and began my Heavenly harkening. Mathematics tells us that when coincidences start coming in quantity, they lose the accidental characteristic of coincidence.

Memorial Day 1955 was warm and muggy. Margaret's son, Trigg, had come over to help me clean house. Nina said she felt slightly strange—not sick, just a bit peculiar—so I made her take it easy all day and she sat in the yard and read. Trigg and I worked hard, and by late afternoon the trailer was shining. Margaret and a friend came by to take us all for a ride.

"Can't I watch TV instead?" the boy asked his mother, and Nina said, "I think I'll stay home with Trigg."

Without them, we took a ride for about an hour to the queer salty lake that gives the city its name. When we returned and pulled into the trailer court, a red police ambulance was standing in front of the Gingerbread House. We saw Trigg outside and called to him, "What's the matter?" and he replied simply, "Nina died."

Shortly after we left he had heard a small moan and turned around to see Nina laying her head back against the pillow behind her on the couch. He jumped over to her and felt her pulse, then dialed the operator and said, "Send a doctor or the police; someone's dying." (This was before the 911 days.) Our little Nina was already gone, her glasses on her nose and a *Time* magazine on her lap—she died quickly and easily, as she would have wanted to.

Mother wrote to me that night, identifying herself by numerous family names, and told me Nina had come gladly and had a happy reunion with her, and with her own mother and father as well. How could I grieve for her after that? At seventy-two, she had just been marking time until she could join her relatives and friends on the other side. But she was my only tie with childhood, and all the family I had left. I felt so lonely without her.

I couldn't help but be thankful, however, that everything seemed to have been arranged in the easiest possible manner for both Nina and me, and the experience didn't faze Trigg at all. Had Nina died alone and I'd walked in on her afterwards, or had I been alone with her when it happened, it would have been terribly upsetting. As it was, resourceful Trigg knew just what to do. The city doctor and the police who came at his call told me they'd never seen a boy of twelve who was so calm and capable in an emergency.

So the disturbing prophecy that we received from the Ouija board in April was fulfilled in May. Nina didn't "love" long.

THIRTEEN

HARVEY TAKES OVER

After Nina's death, Margaret and I decided to go to California to seek our fortunes. I gave notice at the newspaper, and we were ready to leave by late June. During that month I made room in the Gingerbread House for her and Trigg and their quantity of possessions, and they moved in.

When my new trailer-mates arrived, it quickly became evident that the reason Nina and I had gotten along so well together living in our mini-mansion was not any credit to me. It was because Nina was so tiny, so quiet, so adaptable. Margaret spilled over with vitality and ideas. Trigg was interested, inventive, and hyper-energetic. Their parakeet frequently took part in our conversations, and whenever we talked to the bird, Junior was jealous. All this buzzing activity in a twenty-two foot space . . . we're still friends, but—we haven't tried to live together since.

Before our trip, my Chevrolet Bel Air was gone over thoroughly, and we thought it was in shape for pulling the mobile home. A man from the trailer sales company helped us pack for the journey, and he taught Trigg to undo the sewer pipes and electric wires and remove the jacks the trailer sat on. Then everything had to be cleaned thoroughly and stashed inside along with Trigg's bicycle while we were in transit.

It took us all day to pack, and it was late afternoon when we finally started out. I found driving with a trailer in tow enjoyable. It bounded along behind us with a kind of bubbly feejling.

"We can record this in our memoirs as a champagne trip," I said, with spectacular lack of foresight. Evening traffic leaving town proved to be no problem. Everyone gave me a wide berth as I drove slowly at the right side of the main street. If they'd known what a novice was pulling the trailer, they'd probably have climbed telephone poles to get out of our way.

From St. George, Utah, there were eighty-three miles straight across uninhabited desert to Glendale, Nevada. There was nothing in Glendale but a service station and a restaurant, and little else but fifty miles of expanse between it and Las Vegas. As we pulled into a Glendale garage at 8:30 P.M., Margaret, who was driving, commented, "This trailer gets harder and harder to pull." The attendant discovered why. It had a flat tire.

Later we stopped on a hill overlooking the lights of Las Vegas and walked a little way into the desert to be alone with the starry sky; we probably each whispered a word of thanksgiving that the Gingerbread House had had its flat just as we pulled into a garage instead of in this isolated wilderness or on top of one of those desolate pink Utah hills. I hoped Mother was listening, for I couldn't help but wonder if this was an example of how she would be my guardian angel as she had promised.

It's easy to start attributing every favorable act of fortune to supernatural machinations. In order to maintain a basic equilibrium in my life, I have ignored countless incidents that could be added to the string of more-than-slightly-unusual occurrences that keep happening to me all the time. Rest assured that the odd events I do mention are a few among many others forgotten, not recorded in time to be remembered completely, or discarded because noting so many would be tiresome reading.

Drawing into the environs of Los Angeles, we found a trailer camp near the shore in Hermosa Beach. Our big success in California was slow in materializing. Margaret wanted to attend her daughter's wedding in Kentucky, and in a bank box in Maryland lay some of Nina's bonds, which would come in very handy for me almost any day now. So, in a month we were off again, leaving the trailer to await us in California. Driving night and day without air conditioning through an extravagantly hot spell of weather, we soon arrived wilted in Lexington. There Margaret, Trigg and their bird got off, and Junior and I continued on to Oakland alone.

Shortly after I arrived, Margaret wrote that she couldn't return west with me because her mother was sick. I was sorry for my friend, and for her mother—and also just a tiny bit sorry for me, who had to face the trip back alone. Somehow my heart just wasn't in it this time. But the only home I had now was on wheels in California, and my only immediate prospect of making a living was a plan for a movie column, which a Hollywood public relations man was working on for me. So what else was there to do?

I chose the northern route, for its scenery was new to me, and Junior and I were soon enjoying the vastness of the central and western United States. If my guardian angels were ever to be with me, surely they would be there when I was traveling alone, so the idea of their presence was accepted gratefully. And it must be admitted that my dog and my unseen convoy were all splendid traveling companions. If I suddenly decided to go *this* way, nobody gave me any argument about it. Well, actually, Junior—being a dachshund, a breed famous for its independence—was not always a seeing-eye-to-eye kind of dog. But my invisible associates seemed to be in complete accord. There was not a peep out of them, yet they were there when we needed them.

Mt. Rushmore amazed me with its manmade monuments. Yellowstone Park thrilled me with its scenic wonders. In late August, it also nearly froze me to death. After a couple of nights in those log cabins, I left there feeling like a strudel just pulled out of somebody's deep freeze.

The warmth of friendly greetings in Salt Lake City thawed me out, and I remained there for a few days to exchange pleasantries and to sign papers regarding Nina's will. Then I sped onward to sunny California, eager now for my little Gingerbread House.

With all the fantastic climate changes a thousand miles can effect, it was the heat that was unbearable as we drove through the desert toward San Bernardino. Windows rolled down, I kept driving toward the ocean and relief.

Junior had never been so hot in his life. He ran frantically from one side of the car to the other and leaped from the front to the back seat, trying to find nonexistent shade. I became as nervous as he, fearing he'd have a fit or jump out of the car, yet it wasn't possible to hold his busy body and drive too.

Finally I said aloud, "Nina, I know how you loved this little dog. I'm desperate about him right now. Won't you please see if you can quiet him for me?" He *instantly* curled up in the center of the back seat in a spot of brightest sunlight and went to sleep, never stirring until we arrived in Hermosa Beach.

The trailer was awaiting us undisturbed and I moved in, spending days transferring Margaret's belongings into storage. Then I unpacked the household possessions brought from Maryland, having all my own things about me for the first time in a year, exulting at being able to move around in the trailer without bumping into anybody. Loneliness quickly began to invade my little nest, however. I missed Nina's sweetness and Margaret's sunniness and Trigg's brightness.

If only I could get back into contact with Mother again, or if Nina would "write" to me—but nobody answered when I held the pencil lightly in an effort to communicate. Nobody important. Harvey was there sometimes, but just as often as not there was a complete blank. Though this was unpleasant, it was interesting—if it had just been my subconscious mind involved, wouldn't it have written to me when I was lonely and particularly wanted it to?

Then on September 20, Mother popped in for a chat when I picked up the pencil, as casually as if she'd never been out of touch. Good as it was to hear from her, I fussed at her a little, telling her it was awfully hard for me to learn to believe in spirit communication when no spirits would ever communicate. She answered that I had been living such an active life that it was impossible for her to settle me down enough to get anything through my mind, but she assured me she was always on call whenever an emergency arose.

Then Mother suggested something that was to me quite strange. She told me to attend a spiritualist church so that she might be able to give me evidence through a professional medium. This had never occurred to me, partly because of being nonchurch-oriented and partly because at that time I had never thought of spiritualism as anything but a fraudulent farce. (I know better now. There are good and honest spiritualists.) Still, if Mother said so, that was the next step to take.

I picked a church at random from a newspaper ad and attended the next Sunday, eagerly anticipating the promised message. No one there knew me and no identifications were made.

After the service the minister gave a message to each member of the congregation. When it came my time for a reading she said to me, "Who is the old man with the gnarled fingers?"

"Oh, no, not Harvey! I don't want him!" I cried, incensed at his intervention.

The woman smiled, "Yes, he's nodding eagerly to think you recognize him."

That was all she had for me. Asked for news of my mother, the woman's only contribution was a lady bringing me a rose, which could never have been Betty Smith—Betty Smith would more likely have brought me something practical, like a roast beef sandwich.

At home later I gave Harvey the devil when he immediately answered the call of the pencil, smugly self-satisfied because he had produced verification of his reality.

"Why did the medium see you and not Mother?" I asked him.

"Because I pushed in ahead of her."

"That's not fair," I cried. "You know how much I wanted a message from Mother."

My chagrin didn't faze him a bit. He was proud of himself. Lonesome as I was in California, and eager as I was to have evidence of Mother's continued existence so as to be sure my current interests weren't all self-delusion, Harvey had the nerve to brag about forcing his way ahead of her into the minister's line of vision. I hated his guts, in whatever form they existed.

"I don't care if she did see an old man with gnarled fingers like the eighty-year-old carpenter you say you were. I still think you're nothing but an invisible rabbit," I stormed at him. "Just stay out of my life, you jack rabbit!"

FOURTEEN

PAINTING THE
GINGERBREAD HOUSE

I couldn't be sitting around all the time parting the curtain between the spheres. There was my fabulous career to get on with. I called to report back to the public relations man who was going to put my movie column into the big time, and learned that he'd taken a new job and disappeared without even leaving a forwarding address. I phoned the offices of local newspaper editors, discovering their secretaries to be vigilantly protecting them from a columnist who wanted a personal interview instead of merely submitting written samples of her work. All the other contacts I tried to make were just as fruitless.

I never felt so rejected. Sure, people had to be properly seasoned by Hollywood, but it didn't have to happen to me. I wasn't trying to break into the movies.

"So chin up," I chin-upped. "You'll never get anywhere sitting on your big fat chair out here in Hermosa Beach. Get in closer to town where you can at least make a phone call without it costing fifteen cents."

Then I scooted around and found a trailer park in Santa Monica. It was much closer to the hub of activity and had a swimming pool. Arrangements were made to tow the Gingerbread House there immediately.

As the owner of the Hermosa court was pulling us out, there was a loud *wham* as the bottom of the trailer hit the

street going down a hill. Then water began running out the
end of my happy home. It was quickly revealed that the sewer
pipe had rammed up inside and shattered the toilet bowl. The
manager, who was covered by insurance, promised to have it
replaced at once.

The new toilet took over two weeks to arrive, and I had
no water all that time. I was living in the swishest trailer park
in Santa Monica like a hobo in a culvert. The World Series
came to my rescue; I watched it every day on TV and time
passed quickly. When the Dodgers won, I gave a whoop and
a holler that could be heard as far south as San Diego, and
that somehow captivated my neighbors.

Clarence, the widower next door, kindly came to my rescue from then on when any maintenance problems needed
solving. Various others invited me to play bridge. I swam in
the pool every nice day, sunned in my minuscule yard—say,
that was living! I couldn't arouse one jot of interest in trying
to find a job. It seemed that I had an unconscious aversion to
the prospect of high-pressure Hollywood as a place to sink a
taproot.

Then I found a shelf of books about psychical research in
the local library. Discussing the subject with no one, every
night alone I pondered the possibilities, debated the doc-
trines, and marveled at the mysteries the books contained. It
got a little morbid.

When mental activity becomes depressing, getting busy
with my hands is always the solution. I decided to paint my
trailer.

There was certainly no encouragement from the men
around, who all said they'd never undertake it themselves if
they wanted to get anywhere near a professional-looking job.
But my Gingerbread House was beginning to look more like
a boxcar than a dream boat. The cream-colored top was okay,
but the red bottom half was all scratched up. Somehow on
the trip over from Salt Lake City, a tree had gotten too close
to it and its side was peeling. Anyway, the red argued with my

hair every time I stuck my head out the door. I bought two quart-cans of turquoise metal paint and jumped right in.

Observers were very helpful. Clarence thought a finer brush was necessary. Someone else said my paint was too thin. Another thought it was too thick.

"Gimme that brush," the assistant caretaker said, grabbing it out of my hand. Then he slathered on the paint in big strokes as if he were calcimining the side of a barn. It looked awful.

"You'll never get a good job on this," he said, handing the brush back and muttering to himself about women and how stupid they were. I set to work trying to repair the mess he'd made.

Finally, a neighbor was found who knew how to paint on metal. He taught me how to put just the tiniest bit of pigment on the brush and work it in thoroughly until there wasn't a drop or a ripple before adding more. I did it his way, going very slowly and carefully, and the job began to look nearly professional.

How proud I was finishing the first can of paint—a shade of turquoise like sunshine on the ocean off the coast of Florida. I told my kibitzers that the paint in the second can wasn't right, but they all assured me it had to be identical because it was the same lot number. So, I went ahead and used some of it—for touchups here and there. It dried an ugly gray-blue like the ocean in a rainstorm. I returned it to the dealer, waiting over a week with the trailer a two-tone tragedy, while he negotiated with the factory.

One melancholy night, during the time when the paint puzzle was most worrisome, I had a vivid dream that must have been trying to tell me something. It was the first of several easily remembered technicolor dreams, seemingly instigated directly by Mother, that have since come to me during times when encouragement is particularly needed.

In the dream I was driving my car in West Texas and Mother was sitting beside me. There was a lot of water on the highway, and we were aware that there had been big storms in the area. Water crowded the car, ominous cliffs closed in on us and great dark clouds massed overhead. I was frightened. Mother told me to move over and let her drive. As she took the wheel, the cliffs immediately began to recede and the sun came out. The road ahead became a placid lake, the car turned into a boat and we sailed right over the water.

I awoke at six A.M. and lay in bed thinking about the dream. It seemed to mean that I should put myself in Mother's hands so she could pilot me and then everything would be all right. I reached out as usual and turned on the bedside radio. The news broadcaster was saying, "Last night a sudden storm hit West Texas and floods occurred in many areas." Of course, I knew we hadn't really been in West Texas, but it was interesting that even the setting of the dream was realistic.

I wasn't sure just what Mother had in mind, but decided not to worry about the silly old paint . . . or a Hollywood job either. Next day word came from the factory that it would be impossible to match my original shade, but they would be kind enough to replace what I'd used so the trailer could be done over in the new color. I wasn't about to settle for having my home look like a rainy sea. I got out my oil paints and mixed and matched and tinted and tested until the new batch was my original happy turquoise. Three more coats were applied to finish the job.

Five coats of paint on the trailer and one on me, nearly a month of diligent application, and nothing to show for it but success. It looked as wonderful to me as the Blue Boy must have looked to Gainsborough when he stood back to gaze upon his finished masterpiece. It was admired, too, by my neighbors, who rallied 'round with words of praise. The man who'd been the most sure I couldn't do it came to take my picture beside my "Blue Boy" with his color camera, and got my biggest smile for his trouble.

It was just about that time that the library produced a

book entitled *The Reach of the Mind* by Dr. J. B. Rhine, who ran the parapsychology laboratory at Duke University. I'd read about Dr. Rhine and his ESP work at Duke and believed him to be a pioneer in one of the most fascinating and far-reaching new fields of inquiry, but I had somehow not thought of him as being particularly interested in research about the survival of the human soul. I was correct, as I was to learn later, but Dr. Rhine stated in his closing chapter of *The Reach of the Mind* that ESP indicates that man does have a soul, which inevitably leads to the possibility that it might survive death. On page 217 he says, "Any sort of survival of any portion of the personality, for any length of time, holds such significance for human thinking and feeling as to dwarf almost all other scientific discovery by comparison." My sentiments exactly!

"Why, that's the place for me to go to learn more about this," I thought, eager for someone to explain things to me and teach me scientific procedures of research. A letter to Dr. Rhine informed him of my interest in attempting to prove survival and gave him a brief review of my background.

One of his assistants answered encouragingly, and over a period of a month we exchanged correspondence that inspired me to plan definitely to go to Duke—not as a student, but as a guest at the laboratory. Aware that the little bequest Nina had left me wouldn't last forever, or even for long, I hoped to show sufficient aptitude at the parapsychology lab to work into a grant, or else to find some engaging data about which to write.

If the possibility of scientific proof of immortality was such a tremendous stimulus to me, it could also be to others. I didn't know enough about it yet to feel able to draw any conclusions, but my compulsion to learn more on the subject was so strong I was determined to take off for Duke immediately. This, of course, meant trundling my trailer clear across the country, but there being no other way to get it there, I trundled it.

FIFTEEN

TRUNDLING A TRAILER

"You just can't do it alone, Susy," was the opinion of all my neighbors in Santa Monica. None of the women would have dreamed of attempting it, they said. Hands were thrown into the air in horror—all because I was planning to drive my car across the United States from California to North Carolina by myself with a house trailer in tow. This was in the late 1950s and spunky women were more rare than they are today—or were they?

One man was frank enough to say, "I wouldn't even try to pull a trailer that far alone myself, and I don't have the handicap you do."

My main handicap was lack of money; I couldn't afford to hire a truck to pull it for me. I'd gotten along pretty well alone with my game leg and cane. If you can paint a trailer, you can do most anything. Anyway, I didn't expect to be alone. I had my dog.

Anybody else? I wasn't sure. Nothing had been heard via pencil all fall. Even Harvey seemed to have deserted me. Then on the night of December 13, just two days before leaving for the East, I took up the pencil to try to get some last minute encouragement for my trip. Nina began writing. Her word was that she and Mother would be with me all the way and I wasn't to be afraid.

I was buoyed up for several days after Nina's letter and started my journey with confidence. It is just as well I did, for pulling a trailer alone is at best slightly nerve-wracking, and so is Los Angeles traffic. Put them both together and you have an excellent case for staying home and crawling under the bed.

I made it to Indio the first night and drew into a trailer court of sorts, where there was no one to help me get installed. I had to back the Gingerbread House into the plot—something I'd never done before. Now, backing a trailer is no worse than hanging out the wash while balancing yourself on a clothesline in a stiff gale, but it's just as bad. The wheels all turn the opposite way from what you expect, you have a limited space to maneuver in, and like as not you get squeezed up against something in an area impossible to get out of. And then you have to get out.

Once, when I had managed to jam the back bumper of the car tightly against the gas tanks on the front of the trailer, I heard a screeching as if the car had run over six tails of six cats. Not finding any dead cats, or any dents or scratches on either car or trailer, I resumed operations, eventually landing my mobile home in a space sufficiently out-of-the-way that it could remain there overnight.

It was dark and sharply cold by then, and tired and freezing, I sought refuge inside. Dinner by flashlight was a cold meatloaf sandwich accompanied by a fine, dry, distinguished California root beer, served lukewarm. And so to bed, with my clothes on and Junior snuggled against my stomach for warmth.

Not quite the Beverly Hilton.

At six the next morning as I was leaving, my glance just happened to fall on a small piece of bolt on the ground in front of the car. It was turquoise and undoubtedly fell off my trailer, but from where? I finally discovered that the gas tanks were loose. Backing in the night before had sheared off the bolt that secured the tanks to the frame. If my eyes hadn't strayed onto the tiny object on the ground, my tanks might have bounced off in transit. Glancing at the right spot at the right time is one of those things I could easily thank God for, or His invisible cohorts. I was still wary, but it was really an awfully small piece of turquoise-colored bolt.

Not knowing where to have such damage repaired, I stopped at the first business establishment that was open along the highway—a lumber yard. There, a boy put a new bolt on in five minutes and wouldn't charge me for it.

In Yuma, Tucson, and El Paso, I stayed at legitimate trailer courts, but setting up each night and getting organized for living seemed too much effort when all I did was sleep there. In Ozona, a small West Texas town, came a better idea. Actually, it was thrust upon me, because there was no trailer camp or park of any kind in the environs. Finding a good movie, I stopped alongside the curb around the corner from the theater and parked there for the night, enjoyed the picture, cleaned my teeth in the theater rest room, returned home to Junior, who'd retired early, and went to sleep. This was so successful that I continued the procedure most of the rest of my travels, usually driving until dusk and then drawing up by a lighted service station. It was much less trouble and altogether less expensive than trailer courts.

I left Ozona in a heavy fog. The hazy driving didn't bother me particularly, since my unseen Girl Guides were probably out ahead blazing the trail. But as the sun glared forth about nine o'clock in the morning and we picked up some speed over the hills, persistent ideas started bombarding me relating to pulling over to the side of the road.

I said to myself, "Better get my sun glasses out of the glove compartment" and answered, "No, wait until the first roadside park." Because there is also a hand brake to manipulate in order to slow the trailer, as well as the controls of the car to operate it, it was too much effort just to pause alongside the road, and I couldn't reach the glove compartment without stopping. Then I thought, "Really should get some eye drops and use them to wake up more." Again I decided to wait until the next turnout. Right on top of this came the thought that maybe it would be wise to make sure the new bolt was still holding the gas tanks on safely. It all seemed silly, yet the thoughts of stopping were so insistent that finally I pulled over. As the trailer bumped to an unusually jerky halt, I reflected on the dangers of pulling over onto roadside gravel, vowing never to do it again.

Going back to check on the gas tanks and see if those nudges to stop had any significance, I found that the connection plugging the trailer brake into the car's electric outlet had come unhitched and the socket was dragging on the ground! Its prongs were becoming so bent that another few feet of travel would probably have finished their usefulness. Had I tried to go down a steep hill or to stop suddenly without the brake functioning, the Gingerbread House, as well as the car and its occupants, would all have crashed in the nearest ditch.

"Thank you, Mother and Nina," I said with the most fervent conviction yet exhibited. A few more incidents like this and I was going to be firmly dedicated to the principle of guardian angels.

Pondering the necessity to stop a passing motorist to get him to straighten the heavy metal prongs of the plug for me, I thought, "No sir, if there's help in the big things, there's help in the small. There's nothing I can't do alone now—except possibly tango." I opened the trailer, brought out a pair of pliers, applied several ergs of brute force, and fixed the plug myself.

When writing of this incident now, many years later, my dream of Mother helping me with driving problems in West Texas comes to mind. Perhaps that was not only a reassuring dream, but a precognitive one as well.

I spent the holidays in San Antonio, where old friends eased me over Christmas with many warm invitations. I lingered another few weeks to refurbish my little isolation booth with new curtains and pillow covers and a good housecleaning, after which I returned courtesies with a series of small dinner parties. I wanted it known that mobile home living was no tramp existence—and there were converts to my point of view.

I even told a few friends about my new interest in the psychic field. They were attentive and mildly interested. It was mainly a matter of "what crazy thing is Susy into now?" They were patient with me but no fervor was aroused. It has taken recent television shows and movies to make the average citizen eager to hear about these offbeat subjects unless they've had some personal experiences of their own.

Being eager to get to Durham to begin my studies, I soon started out again. At 9:30 A.M. as we were loping along Loop 13 just outside of town, a car suddenly pulled out onto the road not twenty-five feet ahead of me.

I quickly grabbed the trailer's hand brake and stepped on the car's foot brake—everything went out of control at once.

"Help me, help me," I cried frantically as the trailer began to lash the car into a frenzy. The car lunged and jerked the trailer in return and the two were buckling back and forth as they bounded around the highway.

As the gyrations finally ended and we came to a stop facing the opposite direction, I struggled for a moment with excitement, relief and gratitude that the entire kit and caboodle wasn't overturned, then began feeling the unperturbed Junior for broken bones. He'd been knocked off the seat, but our invisible protectors had kept both of us from being hurt. I was ready at that point to quit arguing about my guides' reality. This was an "I believe" moment.

Two men who had seen the accident rushed over to help, and they assured the police who popped up immediately that it had not been my fault. They pulled the trailer off the highway for me and changed the tire that had blown out on the car, refusing anything but a handshake in return. A checkup inside the trailer revealed that everything was strewn about but nothing was broken. When I finally drove off, however, there was a clanking noise in its left wheel. Stops at a filling station and also at a trailer repair shop failed to diagnose the problem. It was suggested that it might be a burned-out bearing and that I should drive along until I found a garage that had a mechanic on duty.

About five miles down the Austin Highway as we clanked along, a truck honked at me and the driver pointed back, so I pulled over off the four-lane turnpike and found a flat on the trailer wheel in question.

Now comes the most unbelievable part of this story, and I offer it as evidence for nothing except good fellowship. A young man named John stopped to help and then gave me his entire day. He first rented an automatic jack from a nearby service station and took the wheel off, discovering that in the wreck, the drum had almost come unriveted from the rim and that another rivet had dropped down inside, ripping the tire.

John put Junior and me and the wheel into his car and took us all back to San Antonio, where we spent the rest of the day waiting while the wheel was welded. We bought a new tire too, and John was even able to get that for me wholesale.

He bought me lunch and a Coke. He never complained about losing his day's trip to Austin, and he told me his life story in an accent so delightfully Texan that I was entertained the whole time. By five o'clock all our chores had been attended to. We returned to the trailer, where John put the wheel back on and started to say goodbye.

"John, it's impossible to thank you," I said. "I've never in my life seen anyone so generous with his time."

"Aw . . ."

"It was way over and beyond the call of duty and goodwill."

"Well, just pass it on. Do a good turn for someone else," he said, and he pulled away, leaving me sitting alone on the highway in the dusk, my eyes damp with gratitude.

I almost didn't start out then. Reaction had been creeping up on me during the day and the temptation was strong to return to San Antonio, at least for the night. Yet like a pilot who has crashed, I must immediately become airborne again or my nerve might desert me entirely, so it was necessary to forge ahead into the deepening shadows. I drove to Austin that night.

Riding along, I couldn't help but recall something Mary Elliott had said in Oakland when I was preparing for my last lonely cruise west.

"I just couldn't do it," she said. "I'd be scared to death."

"Well, do you think I'm not?" I asked her.

SIXTEEN

DUKE, BRIEFLY—ENOUGH IS ENOUGH

My first impression of the parapsychology laboratory at Duke University was wonderful. I arrived in time for the morning coffee hour, when everyone was assembled in the library for their daily biscuit-dunk. All were most gracious during introductions, handsome Dr. J. B. Rhine himself being most prepossessing. As they discussed the morning mail over their coffee and cookies, I sat there all adazzle, overwhelmed that I, a nonentity, was being admitted into this imposing group of academicians.

"I'll never get over being thankful they invited me to come, to sit at their feet as a chela at a guru's," I thought. My eyes popped, too, at all the psychic literature on the library shelves that I could browse. I read constantly from those shelves during my seven weeks in Durham.

But that sitting at feet, that pupil and teacher business— no. That wasn't achieved. I found no gurus in my areas of interest. Here were no fellow parters of the veil. Instead I found myself among scholars and scientists whose goal was to prove extrasensory perception scientifically, but whose intentions were not to get involved in anything that might spoil their other fine work by causing them to receive the label "ghost-chasers." The need was still felt for more evaluations and classifications and analyses and repetitions of former ESP tests, and this is how the laboratory people were spending their time. They accepted me because they hoped I'd fit neatly into the groove and sit myself down with pencil and paper to check columns of precognition symbols.

I tried. Really I did.

But with all the different schools I went to growing up, about half my math training had been missed, and I've ignored simple things like decimals and percents ever since, hoping they'll go away. So I didn't suddenly acquire an aptitude for critical ratios and standard deviations and frequency polygons, and sitting and checking figures is hardly my idea of high tea with the queen. Anyway, if one were going to master clerical work, it should be in order to hold a well-paying job with fringe benefits in a nice office somewhere.

What I stirred up at Duke was a lot of complete indifference. I'd come all the way across the country flying a trailer solo to learn from Duke's experts, but nobody would admit to knowing anything about survival research. If I wouldn't check symbols, all they could do was lead me to the library and place material about the subject before my eager, trembling little mind, with the admonition to be sure to read only "critical" books—those which were entirely "objective" and gave no philosophy and carried no message.

I have come to be tremendously grateful to the laboratory people for this introduction in strict objectivity, realizing that it was the best possible thing they could have done for me. Too many books in this field are pointless because their authors accept everything they see and experience at face value. Because of my lifetime of arguing with concepts, my journalistic skepticism, and the indoctrination in critical evaluation received during my time at the parapsychology laboratory, I have been able to maintain a more objective approach to my subject in all my writing with Mother and later with James.

Those critical volumes I read gave me an insight into the accepted way to evaluate phenomena objectively. One should always beware of errors of memory, observation, narration, and inference before accepting any allegedly supernormal experience as valid. I reconsidered my own events with this in mind. I was sure there were few errors of *memory* because of my habit of writing down everything unusual the day it occurred—even incidents happening en route, like the flat in front of the garage in the middle of the Nevada desert and the mental warnings that caused me to discover the unplugged trailer brake.

I was fairly confident that my newspaper training helped me to make only slight errors, if any, in *observation or narration,* but what about the errors of *inference* proper researchers were so wary of? Would attributing my series of unusual events to spirit intervention be any less rational than ascribing them to coincidence, chance, Heavenly miracles or a continued although repressed psychological dependence upon a dominating mother?

I learned that Dr. Rhine and his wife, Dr. Louisa Rhine, had expressed themselves firmly as convinced that there was not one iota of evidence that automatic writing ever came from anything other than the writer's subconscious mind. So I was faced with the fact that nothing I might say or think would be of any concern or value to anyone at the lab unless powerful evidence could be produced.

Determined to produce it, I tried to write automatically most evenings, but with only picayune results. Nonetheless, I pushed on in my naive effort, trying night after night to establish a smoothly functioning communication system with my invisibles so that they could give me something so evidential it would *have* to prove survival to my Durham associates. I wasn't successful. Harvey invariably intruded at least once into every letter.

Well, if I couldn't communicate, books were still available. I prowled the library all the more fervently, carrying home stacks of volumes every night. There was nothing else to do, so I read constantly, trying to encompass everything possible about the subject—everything properly scientific, that is. Much of the reading was morbid, even though it consisted only of case histories carefully attested to by numerous witnesses.

I sat cooped up alone in my turquoise-colored ivory tower, huddling near the fire and reading about phantoms, hallucinations, and apparitions. There was no one to talk with and the principal ingredients of my life were rain and pain in the Carolina winter dampness. How miserable can you get?

Then one night while cleaning my teeth, I glanced up at the skylight over my shower and there a ghostly face grimaced at me. Its wrinkled visage looked so much like an old man's that it could be suspected that Harvey had at last learned the art of materialization. Common sense said no, and daylight revealed that what appeared to be facial features were actually leaves and twigs dropped on the outside of the glass. But from then on my shower curtain was kept pulled at night so "he" couldn't leer at me. It became evident to me that unless I was very careful, in my depressed existence I might let myself become overly emotional.

That did it. I ran for advice to Professor Hornell Hart of the sociology department at Duke, who had recently addressed the laboratory people and admitted his belief in survival after death. Dr. Hart had enough personal psychical experiences to make him aware that there is a great deal more to this subject than meets the eye of a merely dispassionate, critical scientific observer.

When asked for help, Dr. Hart gave it freely. It was he who put all the conclusions I'd halfheartedly reached into a usable philosophy adaptable for my needs, starting me on the road to adjusting myself to my peculiar situation. He did not think I was misguided and suggested I was obviously receptive to assistance from the spirit world. He asserted that it should be put to use not just as a phenomenon with which to try to convince unbelievers, but as an inspirational thing in my life that would radiate inner peace.

I had all the ingredients for contentment, but instead of using them I'd been fighting them and arguing with them and trying to prove them to the satisfaction of others instead of myself. When I started trying Dr. Hart's suggestions, all the pieces of the puzzle fell into place, creating a beautiful, jubilant happiness that glowed within me for quite a while. In fact, although it's quieted down a bit with age, it's with me still.

Dr. Hart recommended that instead of trying for more active physical communication, I make an effort to achieve silent, passive awareness of Mother's presence. Via pencil she later agreed: "Try to be receptive. Try to attain true relaxation and elevation of your mind. You are closer when you reach out to me."

I made a conscious effort at projecting and expanding and surging mentally, and there was a wonderful feeling of intimacy with Mother, and also with Nina (who seems to have remained for only a few days after Dr. Hart got me straightened out, and then left to work on her own development by staying with another friend who needed help).

I learned to feel close to Mother by being mentally aware, instead of by actively trying to communicate. This was much more successful, for there were not so many frustrations. She had told me I had only to be receptive and all the love and aid a guardian angel could give would be available, and now I was finally willing to accept it wholeheartedly. Even though I yet argued and rationalized and quibbled with the evidence and knew I always would, still . . .

I had peace at last, and it seemed that it might be possible to retain it.

SEVENTEEN

RETURN TO WARMTH

After the squeeze they had gotten me into, it seemed better to leave those psychic books alone for a while, and anyway, I was becoming so rain soaked in Durham I was in danger of breaking out any day with mushrooms, so it appeared wise to go somewhere else. I had begun to feel that there might be something worth writing about, after all, in my experiences. I though Bill Hanemann, who used to write those high-powered editorials for *Shopping with Susy* in Daytona Beach, might be able to help me whip it into readability with his invaluable suggestions. A couple of days after my talk with Dr. Hart, I hitched up and started for Florida.

I'm sure I wasn't missed at the parapsychology lab. Let's face it: Susy Smith was a gimpy woman who walked with a cane and lived in a small house trailer in a muddy park. If I'd been cagey enough then to call myself Ethel Smith-Smith and had been driving the good-looking Cadillac I was later to buy secondhand, I would have appeared more likely to have money or prestige to contribute to their organization.

When I visited the lab years later, after I'd become the founder and president of the Survival Research Foundation, Dr. Rhine invited me into his private office for a chat and practically gushed over me.

Never having hauled a trailer in the rain, I drove south slowly and carefully, riding for two days in a constant downpour. But the car soon took the bit in its teeth and started speeding with eagerness toward warmth and sunshine again. The first faint whiffs of Florida smelled like Arpège to me as we flitted across that fragrant, flowering state.

It was in a palm-shaded trailer park in Holly Hill, on the river just above Daytona, that we settled down. There Junior and I began adjusting our shape into a design for peaceful living after all our recent travel and travail. Time was passed visiting with friends, reading, listening to concertos on my record player, swimming or hiking with my dog on the beach, playing bridge and basking in the sunshine attended by caroling mockingbirds. Existence had never seemed lovelier.

Impressed by my serenity, others were eager to learn what precious substance I had mined in the West.

"Whatever happened to you?" they said, and, "Where did you get that spark?"

So I told them. The more I talked about it, the more it was revealed that some could go me two or three better—phenomena-wise. Until one begins to speak freely of psychic experiences, one just isn't aware that so many people have them. They may have a precognitive dream that came true or a telepathic episode, or they may see ghosts as a matter of habit—the point is that they rarely mention it for fear of being misunderstood. When they discover someone they are sure won't laugh at them, they are eager to discuss the strange things that happen to them.

Yet as I mentioned earlier, people in general have not shown interest unless they've had their own experiences. It is only within the last five years or so that there is real enthusiasm for the supernatural.

I asked about local mediums, eager to attend any sessions available. There was always the chance that professional sensitives might be able to give me more authentic evidence of survival than anything I could achieve alone. I made it a habit for years afterward to case mediums in each new community I visited, taking careful shorthand notes of everything they told me. A glance over my records reveals that much of what was received was hit or miss, but some of it was exceptional.

My first Florida experience with a medium was with Mrs. Springstead in Daytona Beach. She was small, plump and pretty, and her specialty was psychometry. Psychometry is the faculty of divining knowledge about an object, or about a person connected with it, by holding that object. One possible explanation of why it works is that everything has a force field around it that retains impressions.

A basket was passed around and members of the audience were asked to place personal belongings in it. Springstead then took rings or watches or billfolds at random from the basket and gave messages to their owners, who were unidentified until she asked them to claim the object at the end of her reading.

I went in as a stranger and did not say anything to anyone except, "How do you do." But when Springstead picked my ring out of the basket, she said that its owner had excellent spirit influences around her. Then she said that my mother was informing her that we had communication via automatic writing.

"You have a wonderful mother who says that you talk to her frequently," she said, "but she just wishes you could hear her answer you. She's eager to make you see her, and she hopes to show herself to you someday."

(Later at home, I said, "Mother, if you ever do find yourself able to become visible, *please* don't do it unless some skeptical person is with me who can see you too, or I'll go completely *mad* trying to tell people what happened without a witness to verify it.")

Springstead then said, "You make your living in your own home," which seemed to me fairly accurate, since I had once again determined to become a professional writer. Then she asked, "Does Texas mean anything to you?" Not waiting for an answer she continued, "I'm told that San Antone, Texas, is closely associated with you."

"It's the city where I was raised," I replied. Then she said my work would be successful with Mother's assistance. That was all she gave me, but it was enough.

I knew one thing for sure. She had not been reading my mind, for nowhere even in my most elemental depths could she have dredged up the pronunciation, "An*tone*." No self-respecting former resident of San Antonio would tolerate San An*tone* for one minute.

The next Sunday found me at a different church, where I received only the brief message that an older man with a beard was with me. I thought, "That damned Harvey again." But she went on to say that the man looked like me from the nose up. She added, "He's related to you. You have a picture of him at home." The only picture at home of an older male relative with a beard was of my great-grandfather. I guess you could say there is a family resemblance, especially in the wave of his hair, that was auburn just like Mother's. But I tossed this off with the thought, "Who knows the resourcefulness of that Harvey. Now he's claiming to look like me."

Disappointed with my message, I didn't slip any money into the basket which was passed around for a "love offering." I didn't have that much affection for a medium seeing Harvey. And then to proclaim a resemblance! That was getting to be just a bit too much.

I returned to the Gingerbread House and took pencil in hand for my evening attempt at a chat with Mother. (Yes, it was still a regular custom I hadn't been able to give up, despite Dr. Hart's advice.) Harvey started writing as usual and said, "Your mother is not here." I asked if it were he the medium had seen, fully expecting the same smug affirmative he'd given me last fall in Los Angeles, but this time he said, "No."

"Who was it then?"

"Your great-grandfather."

"That's hard to believe."

"But," he wrote, "it's true." Then I insisted again that he let Mother write. He pestered me a few minutes longer, however, and then the pencil very forcibly wrote "Anderson."

I doubted if either Harvey or Mother, or my subconscious mind, would have thought of Grandpa Anderson by just his last name that way. I asked, "Who is writing?"

The answer came: "I'm your mother's grandfather."

"Was it you the medium saw tonight?"

"It was."

"Can you identify yourself further?"

"I'm Robert Ingram Anderson."

"Where did you live?"

"Oakland, Maryland."

"Is there anything special you want to talk to me about?"

"It is anything of which there is a question."

Just then Harvey pushed in with his silly, "I love you, Harvey" and other ineptitudes. After several attempts to dislodge him in that battle of wills it was apparently necessary to wage with him, Grandpa wrote again: "It is Anderson now."

"Is it really you?"

"I'm really Grandpa."

"When will we ever get rid of Harvey?"

"Only when we are able to teach him, but he is a primitive person."

"What can I do about him?"

"You must not ever let him write to you. When he starts, you must cease writing at once. It is the only way it will be conquered."

"Are you sure this is the only way?"

"Yes, it is true."

After that Harvey took over and I couldn't get Grandpa again. I thought it was noticeable how differently he had expressed himself from the way Mother wrote. She always spoke as simply as possible, but his style was stilted and he used words like "cease," "primitive," "conquered." And he identified himself as "your mother's grandfather" instead of as my great-grandfather, as I thought of him.

Naturally I wondered if the medium had just mentioned a man with a family resemblance—everyone has such in the spirit world—and my subconscious mind (that poor old catchall that had been catching all the blame for so long) had come up with an answer in producing Grandpa by automatic writing. Role-playing by the subconscious mind is said by some critics to be the explanation for all the different characters a medium produces. Somehow this didn't sound too convincing to me in the light of everything else that had happened—although as an isolated incident, that certainly would have been the interpretation to accept.

Then another possibility occurred to me—that perhaps my great-grandfather had often been visiting this descendant whom he'd never met in the flesh, but couldn't make himself known and wasn't able to write to her until she became aware of his presence from some outside source. Since then several psychics have given me the name Robert; and in 1965 in Seattle, Washington, medium Keith Milton Rhinehart told me definitely that a grandfather named Robert was my guide who stays with me. Keith gave me some personal information purporting to come from this Robert that nobody was likely to have known by normal means. This made me feel more secure about my earlier experience when Robert Ingram Anderson allegedly communicated by automatic writing.

I decided to return to this Daytona medium who had produced a relative buried fifty-four years ago to see if she could help me to remove Harvey. She gave me an afternoon appointment at which I immediately explained my problems with my rude intruder. When she asked me to write to him, he eagerly participated as soon as I picked up the pencil, glad to be the center of attention. Then the medium announced that she could see Harvey. She gave him a little lecture and threatened to set her Indian spirit guides on him if he didn't behave and let me write without interference.

The idea that native Americans are so frequently used as guides seems far-fetched to many people, but because they were so close to nature while on Earth, deceased Indians are said to have more etheric power. Actually, in the days before the white man came with his corruptions, all great braves were mystics, commonly inducing trance and visions by prayer, fasting and lonely vigil. Whether we understand it or not, many psychics claim to have contact with Indians, primarily as bodyguards to keep spirit intruders away.

As I'm writing this book in 1999, I ask my own guide what they prefer to be called. "Native American" he said, but mediums may still refer to them as Indian guides. He feels there is no stigma attached to a word used for such a long time.

This medium told me that she could hear Harvey's answer to her threat. "What can Indians do to hurt me?" he asked with his usual flippancy. "They can't kill me."

She thought they could run him off, though, so she invoked their aid. I went home reasonably reassured. I didn't try any writing for a whole week after that, confident the venerable braves had done their good deed, but reluctant to find out. When my pencil was picked up again in the loose way that indicated my willingness to palaver, Harvey was still there, boasting, "I'm not afraid of Indians." When assured that because of his meanness I would have to give up automatic writing altogether, he wrote, "You won't stop."

"Yes, I will."

"No, you won't."

I said, "Harvey, you're bad. You'll have a terrible time always if you don't learn to behave better."

He replied, "You'll come over and all will be well."

"Why, you don't think for one moment I'll have anything to do with you after I die?"

"You'll have to."

"I'm forced to give up writing because of you," I said regretfully.

"Not true," he wrote.

"For the last time before I stop altogether, will you let Mother write to me?"

"No."

So unleashing the Indians on him didn't remove Harvey. Well, I didn't doubt either their bravery or their power, if there really had been any Indians there at all. Maybe there just weren't enough of them to take on a tough old bird like Harvey. There's always the chance that he might have been an Indian fighter himself back in the early days of the Wild West and knew a few tricks of his own. So I just gave up with Harvey, planning to try to cope with him some other time, when maybe a more formidable tribe could be assembled to send after his scalp.

Or . . . if it were only possible to get word to his wife that he was here chasing this redhead.

EIGHTEEN

THE TYPEWRITER
GETS INTO THE ACT

My Daytona friends' interest in the stories I told of my efforts to communicate with my mother inspired me to work on a written account of it. So I started steadily telling it all to my typewriter.

One day it talked back.

At a loss for words, I slumped in my chair to relax, letting my fingers lie lightly on the typewriter keys.

"I wish I knew what I was talking about," I said aloud. Then my hands began to type slowly, seemingly of their own volition. What they wrote was as different from what I wanted to say as popcorn is from peanut butter.

I didn't like my typewriter making light of my dignified ideas this way. My book was supposed to have significance, yet here it was being told not to take itself so seriously. Don't push your conclusions at your reader, my typewriter intimated. Splash him with drops from your font of inspiration and let him brush them off or absorb them as he wishes.

After the initial surprise at being given an argument by this mechanical busybody, it suddenly dawned on me that Mother had found a way to communicate again. We hadn't tried automatic writing by pencil since I had lowered the boom on Harvey, but had been satisfied with mental communion instead.

Now she was voluble again—apparently I was relaxed enough that she could get through to me on the typewriter—and she was indicating her interest in working on the book with me. I was delighted, and took the occasion to ask her to answer many questions that had been occurring to me. One was this guardian angel business.

"I really am your guardian," she wrote. "I protect you. If you will keep yourself receptive to the thoughts I send you, success can be yours, for together we can build for you a life of happiness and accomplishment."

"But, Mother, don't you have anything more important to do than hang around with me?"

"You are the most important thing in the world to me," she answered. "But anyway, this is my work as well as my pleasure. As part of our development we must stay with someone to help him, and naturally I chose you."

In some of her initial typewritten messages, Mother spoke of the fact that guardian angel relationships could be very pleasant, particularly if those on Earth could know of their assistant's presence and acknowledge it. If it's someone you were very close to, you frequently can feel his proximity even if you have not tried to develop your sensitivity, and when you think you have a feeling of his or her presence, be happy about it. I realized I'd had wonderful evidence of Mother's guardianship already and would continue to add to it whenever possible.

There were many instances of what seemed more than chance to me in the answers Mother gave me. For example, at the start of the book I was writing an account of Mother and Daddy's childhood adventures. He had run away from his Aunt Mabel's home in his teens (she raised him after his mother died when he was ten) because she was mean to him. Hoping to get to California hoboing on a freight train, he hid in a boxcar that turned out to have two empty telephone-cable spools in it. They rolled back and forth all night from one end of the jouncing car to the other. He couldn't get a moment's rest, so he danced a *something* all night. I wanted an obscure word that would not intrude, but *Roget's Thesaurus* didn't have one that wasn't too traditional. I asked Mother for a good word and she wrote on my typewriter "rigadoon."

"Don't you mean 'brigadoon'," I asked. "That's not a dance."

"Look it up," my fingers typed, so I did. The dictionary revealed a word so little known it wasn't even in *Roget's*: "Rigadoon—a lively dance with a peculiar jumping step. It is no longer popular." Well, it was popular with me, because I thought this was pretty darn good evidence.

Bill Hanemann, who was presiding over my writing in the capacity of chief consultant on grammar, rhetoric, and "Susy, for Christ's sake, why can't you *ever* learn the difference between 'lie' and 'lay'?" was finding his mordant Hollywood-conditioned mind occasionally disturbed by some of the things with which he was being confronted.

One day he was twitting me as usual about my etheric enthusiasms.

"If you're going to believe all this twaddle, I'd like some personal evidence," he said. "Maybe it's catching after all."

"All right. I'll ask Mother to tell us what you're thinking this very minute." I put my fingers on the machine. Nothing happened. Bill and I discussed the fact that even if we got what was on his mind, it wouldn't necessarily be evidence of survival, just testimony for the existence of telepathy—but still supernormal one way or another. Still nothing happened. Then the typewriter wrote, "Yes, I know what he was thinking, but I'm not able to tell you now. Wait until you're not trying so hard."

Bill, of course, thought this was a cop out.

Two nights later, after my fingers had been beating the keys for several hours receiving information about her world from Mother, I said, "Reception's as good now as it ever is; see if you can tell me what Bill was thinking the other day when we put you on the spot."

"A picture of you," she typed.

"What picture?" I asked, my mind busily trying to remember some photograph Bill might have seen. Naturally my thoughts got in the way of her reply.

Finally Mother sighed—I know very well that she sighed—and wrote, "You won't let me say what I want to. Just tell Bill he was thinking about a picture of you and let it go at that."

The next time my severest critic dropped by I said, "Were you thinking of a picture of me the other day?" He gave me a startled stare. In fact, it was several minutes before he regained his composure sufficiently to tell me that just at the time I had said, "I'll get Mother to tell me what you're thinking" a ray of sunshine had come through the slats of the Venetian blind and had hit my red hair in such a way that he had wondered if it would be possible to catch it with color film. He was a photography buff and enchanted by unusual effects.

After Bill considered my message a few minutes he began to back out of it, as those who are trying to be strictly objective almost always do. (I myself have done this often.) Maybe his lips had unknowingly whispered the words "picture of Susy" without either of us hearing him, and my subconscious mind had picked it up. Maybe I had unconsciously lip read it. We go very far afield when we try to account for some of these incidents by reaching for explanations that do not involve the supernormal. Maybe, he finally concluded, there is such a thing as *delayed* telepathy.

"Or maybe I just happen to have an unusually bright typewriter," I said with the slightest touch of sarcasm.

No use arguing with him about it, though. Why *should* he believe I was corresponding with a mother who'd been dead for seven years? For Bill the trouble was that he was never able to find another explanation for the incident that made any more sense than the survival hypothesis. He decided the safest thing to do was to ignore it.

Soon there was another interesting exchange of this nature. My friend Irene Kellogg was in a hurry for a picture of a dove of peace that she needed as a model for a float the Pilot Club was entering in a forthcoming parade. But she couldn't find one, and her committee was ready to start decorating. She bewailed her problem over the phone.

"Maybe there's something here," I suggested. "I'll ask Mother." I went back to my typewriter and Mother wrote that we had exactly what Irene needed if she could just tell me where it was. Since I was sure the only place we could have such a picture was in a magazine or book, several highly colored answers came giving pages and issues, which revealed instead the faces of foreign diplomats or advertisements for cars or recipes for elaborately gooey cakes.

Just then a neighbor dropped in, and when told I was trying to get a message from my mother, she wanted to make use of my talented typewriter for her own needs.

"Ask my husband if I should sell my trailer," she said, so I wasted valuable time from my dove hunt trying for a reply that would amaze and convert Mrs. Thripp.

Mother wouldn't cooperate at all with this delay. My fingers wrote nothing while I was trying to receive word for my neighbor; but finally an abrupt, "Get dove for Irene," was typed. I continued talking to my guest, however, my fingers resting idly on the keys. After a few minutes, while we waited but got nothing, the typewriter wrote, rather crossly, it seemed to me, "You are not doing this right. Ask Mrs. Thripp to come back later."

When the lady left and I was back to giving Mother my full attention, the answer came quickly: "My autograph book." I found the album from her high school days in a carton in the trunk of the car, where it had been stored since the year before, and in it were two big doves with olive branches in their beaks—the sort of sugar-coated pictures that used to be on valentines. They were exactly what Irene needed. After we'd seen the parade a few days later, we agreed that Irene's dove was the best thing in it, and Irene told everyone Susy's mother was responsible.

Yes, I had seen those doves in Mother's album from time to time, possibly even when packing the album in the carton before leaving Oakland the previous August. I can't say positively that my subconscious was not recalling that they were there, so this isn't offered as proof of communication. Yet to me it is of value because of the way it illustrates how Mother maintained her own persevering character, even interrupting me when she felt it necessary to do so.

She was always so consistently herself in her communications, expressing her own personality, having her own normal reactions to things. They are seldom like mine, but invariably like hers. If I tried to give her credit for powers she didn't have, she corrected me. She made no claim to being Superman, although with my lack of knowledge about conditions in her sphere, I was often tempted to expect her to act like him. What is even more convincing, she refuses to accept credit for every act of friendly fortune in my life, which I'm likely now to attribute to my guardian angel.

One night I had a pot roast in the pressure cooker. The instructions said to cook it for half an hour, but within twenty minutes such a savory smell was assailing me that I was afraid the meat would burn. So I asked Mother, "Is my roast done yet?"

There was a brief pause; then she typed, "Not quite."

"How much longer will it take?"

She completely surprised me with her reply: "I don't know. I never used a pressure cooker." It was true. Mother had died before we got ours.

Mother helped me every day as I wrote, and then she decided that conditions were good enough that she could start dictating a special chapter of her own to explain immortality. We put the reminiscences aside and wrote at a rapid clip about her world. I sat there hour after hour trying to make my mind a blank as she wrote through me, yet still aware of every word that was written. She claimed that this was beneficial, even if more difficult for us both, because if the information were received incorrectly, she could tell me and I could make the necessary changes.

"No, that's not right; fix it" was her most frequent interruption, as day after day, night after night, we polished each sentence and each paragraph until she was satisfied with them.

Mother, in what I have always referred to as her chapter, gave a summary of all the material James was later to elaborate upon. At the time "Mother's Chapter" was written, there were assuredly various invisible ones who were helping her get the information into my head and through my fingertips. It does not surprise me that the writing style of all the alleged communicants sounds similar no matter who is purporting to write, and also that it sounds somewhat like my style when I try to write with dignity. It must be remembered that it has all been filtered through my mind, no matter how much I have tried to keep my thoughts from coloring it. But I don't *know* all this information—how could it possibly have been unconsciously instigated by me?

The communicants have stated that the reason they could impart philosophy through me is because I had no firmly held notions about philosophical or religious concepts. This, they explained, was what made me especially useful to them as a channel—I would not distort their material with my own opinions.

The fact that I am awake and somewhat alert when typing is also said by the communicants to be an advantage, because I can then be critical about the wording of the information received and ask about anything that doesn't seem to make sense or is confusing or unclear. They do not object to my querying them, for it is my own reception I am questioning, not the validity of their information.

I have also been told that the reason the team of Betty Smith and her daughter was used is that our characters are in some ways so much alike, particularly in our stubborn desire and determination to do things as well as possible and to stick to them until we accomplish our goals. The following chapter, I believe, was written by my mother.

NINETEEN

MOTHER'S CHAPTER

The conscious spirit of each individual born on Earth eventually achieves unity with God. I do not mean the anthropomorphic "like a man" God of Earth conception, for that attempts to limit to a force that which cannot be limited, is inconceivable in its infinity. God instead is the state of highest awareness, power most superlative, illimitable love, infinite consciousness.

When each spirit attains his highest development, he is incorporated into this great ultimate, which is God, yet he still retains his individual personality and identity. This can be understood when one thinks of the ocean, which is increased by every molecule of water that enters it, and yet upon analysis each molecule is found to maintain its own individuality.

The same natural laws that systematically bring the flowers into bloom and the trees into leaf and that cause the planets to move in their orbits also cause each consciousness, from the instant of its inception in an Earth body, inevitably to continue its movement forward until it finally achieves the ultimate, although the free will of each individual controls the length of time his progress will take.

Usually, when a man dies, a spirit who has his interest at heart welcomes him and explains that he has passed through the experience called death, but that actually he is still alive,

and that he has maintained his conscious individuali
out its being in any way changed. He is told that he no...
himself in the etheric plane, which is coexistent with the
Earth plane, but in a different dimension. He is informed
that although he has shed his Earth body he has retained its
etheric counterpart of identical appearance, but of another
substance; that his conscious spirit will always continue to
live, passing through numerous planes of existence, with
advancement depending upon his own efforts.

It is made clear to the new arrival that he will have assistance constantly along the way, but that no one can force him
to choose the right path; the decision is entirely up to him.

He is told that all his talents must be used, and that his
innate capabilities for love, forgiveness, compassion, reasonable-
ness, mercy, tenderness, sincerity, generosity, kindness, courage,
patience, justice, tolerance, unselfishness—all the character-
building virtues—must be increased to their highest degree
before he may proceed out of the etheric. He cannot leave that
plane no matter how long it's been, until this is accomplished
by his own conscious effort.

Now the kind of man who was aware of his personal
responsibility for spiritual growth and who recognized his
obligation to love his fellow men will experience in the etheric constant forward progress, and as his character improves, so
do the surroundings in which he finds himself. There is great,
unimaginably great, beauty here, but it can be seen only by
those who have achieved awareness of it. It will be possible for
this enlightened spirit to live in a sublime world, to hear and
appreciate splendid music, to spend his time occupied by
enjoyable tasks among friendly companions, including many
he loved most while on Earth. The spirit who goes upward
indeed lives in paradise.

But if his nature was mean and weak, he will exist in sor-
did, dismal surroundings, which become increasingly more
dreary until he sees the error of his thinking, for each spirit
makes with his thoughts the conditions in which he lives.

It is possible to go through an entire Earth life without developing any of one's capabilities, or even facing up to the need to do so. Heredity and environment play a large part in one's natural inclination toward or away from self-improvement, but no man is accountable for more than he is potentially capable of achieving. However, anyone who makes an effort to learn to love his fellow men and to gain wisdom has a more successful life on Earth and is further advanced when he reaches the next plane. It is an eventual necessity in world progress that more and more people be reared with awareness of the importance of character development. It is much easier to build it on Earth than after death and a great deal of time and misery later will be saved if you have begun your progression before you die.

Sometimes it takes many hundreds of years before some especially closed-minded spirits can be made to understand the need to start their own personal strivings, and often its urgency almost never can be learned. Even persons of intelligence, if their minds are corrupted by hatred, may be blindly unwilling to accept the fact that their own endeavors—nothing else—will get them out of the low spiritual state they are in.

The average person during his life on Earth is so preoccupied with making a living, raising a family and trying to accumulate material benefits that almost no time is spent on conscious efforts to improve. Although he doubtless leads a life of *some* service, whatever discipline he acquires is purely coincidental, for he does not take advantage of the fact that the problems he has to face are challenges which present him with the opportunity to strengthen his character. He manages to increase some of his good qualities to some extent; he steps forward and he backslides; he does something really fine and then something futile or inept. When he dies, this man already has some quantitative development. It is not difficult for him to be convinced that his future progress in the spirit world is up to him.

If he accepts this and begins to work on himself, informed spirits will give him as much time and instruction

as he needs along the way. An entirely new underst
necessary, for everything is instigated and accom
this plane by thought power. Even movement from one pla
to another is done by thinking of where you wish to be, and
with sufficient concentration, you suddenly find yourself
there. All character building is consciously motivated, and
you must decide upon the course of action that will enable
you to improve each of your capabilities, and then act on
your decisions.

Usually your first step is to stay close to someone on
Earth who requires assistance in the very virtues you need to
improve. The only way you can help this person is with your
thoughts, but if they are positive enough and strongly enough
held, you can frequently give substantial assistance.

It is much easier to guard your speech and your actions
on Earth than to try in the spirit world to correct harm you
have done. It is also less difficult to follow the golden rule
than to make retribution, for if you have done anyone an
injury during your life, then when your progression starts
after death you will feel obligated to remain with that person
until you've made recompense.

Of course, assistance may be given to loved ones, and
most spirits become companions or guardian angels to those
on Earth they care for, impressing their minds with advanta-
geous thoughts whenever possible.

Unfortunately, sometimes those who die are in such a
state of degradation and moral ignorance that they will not
pay attention to these helpful spirits. Without previous
knowledge of what to expect after death, they may not even
be aware that they have died and so think that what they are
experiencing is just a bad dream. But if they will listen, the
informed spirits who make it their practice to rescue these
newcomers will tell them the truth, and their future success
is assured without too great a delay.

Frequently, however, men and women who die in an
unenlightened state will not accept what is told to them.

Thinking they are already in Heaven or Hell, depending upon what they had conceived to be their prospects, they will consider no other possibility, and they remain in the same ignorant condition, making no effort to improve. These are the people it is most urgent to reach with the truth before they die.

No other thing that man can do to man is as bad as murder, which liberates a soul who is probably totally unprepared to progress. Capital punishment is just as wrong, because it allows to enter the spirit world one with hate and revenge in his heart. You do not destroy an enemy by killing him, you merely unleash him in another and invisible form. One who murders must spend so much time in the next plane undoing his wrongs that there is nothing but Hell for him for seeming eons of time. To kill a person is the worst thing you can do, and to kill yourself is just as bad.

It is necessary to learn to love one another before it is possible to progress, for without love little growth can be attained. Despite the mental discipline it demands, this necessary trait should be developed as highly as possible before one dies.

I am not advocating a thing impossible to do. Jesus did it as an example for all. In fact, many have lived only for others, and their lives have been examples for the world to follow. Those who have revered humanity have been the most successful of all men. St. Paul, Moses, St. Francis of Assisi, Siddhartha Gautama (Buddha), Florence Nightingale, Jane Adams, William and Evangeline Booth, Abraham Lincoln, Clara Barton, Mahatma Mohandas Gandhi and Albert Schweitzer are only a few of the many who have devoted themselves to helping mankind.

The lives of these men and women illustrate that it is possible for happiness to be found in selflessness. But the entreaties of all religions that men learn to love their brothers have never been embraced by the world as a whole. They've been rejected because people thought they were meant for others rather than for themselves. They've been overlooked because life seemed complete enough without them. They have not been followed because it appeared too difficult.

There is no quick or easy way to learn goodwill toward humanity, but the first step is taken when one begins to see the need of it. Since all are enduring the same struggles and learning the same lessons and trying for the same goals, it should not be difficult to attain a feeling of kinship and compassion for them. To think kindly of others will be easier when it is realized that each must eventually become aware of the necessity to progress. For if you know this, and the one who injures you does not, then you can pity that soul for the lack of understanding of the monumental task ahead. Instead of hating, forgive. Think to yourself, "God bless him," and then forget the grievance.

The way to learn to improve yourself is this: know first that thoughts are actual things. Then you can realize that every negative thought that enters your mind must be denied and a positive thought substituted for it so that the power that the negative thought exerts may be canceled by a positive power immediately put into play.

It is laborious to do this at first, but it will grow easier with practice, until finally the reaction of denial to any negative thought will become instinctive. The substitution of a positive thought will also become a matter of habit. Soon you will notice evidence of the progress you have made and the improvement in your life because of it. When friends begin to ask what it is that has brought that glow of happiness to you so constantly, you will suddenly realize that a constructive force is revealing itself continuously in your life, and you will know such peace as you previously would not have believed possible.

Those who call you ingenuous if you try to live by the golden rule will have a much more difficult time than you will in the etheric. They are the ones who are really naive, because their minds are closed to the real delights of life. Only when one begins to master himself, instead of deceiving himself by believing his mediocre existence to be satisfactory, will he know what real joy is. For there is such pleasure in each contact, such harmony of mind, that all friction disappears.

Love of mankind could be learned easily if it were taught to children so they would be raised with it always in their hearts. Too many adults don't implant the importance of tolerance. They train their children by precept to hate and belittle others instead of insisting that it is necessary to have brotherly love for everyone no matter how misguided or ignorant, or how different in race or color or habits. If it were learned in childhood, then it would not be so difficult for the adult to practice as a part of his habitual thinking.

It is unfair to raise children who do not know about the necessity to attain wisdom, it is a disservice to them to allow them to grow up without inner harmony or awareness of the significance of achieving it, and if they discover after death that their entire lives on Earth have been practically wasted because so little character was built, it is hard for them not to feel that their parents were neglectful, no matter how indulgent they seemed to be at the time. It is too late then to learn these lessons from life's experience, and there is nothing to do but start in the etheric with whatever slight amount of spiritual development one has and build upon that.

Each baby comes into the world as a consciousness (or soul or ego or spirit) wearing a body as it would a coat. It lives on Earth for one purpose—to establish its identity and then use life's experiences to acquire wisdom, build character and attain individual stature. When the body is discarded at death, the consciousness continues in spirit dimensions until perfection is achieved.

Advanced personalities may remain in the etheric plane for as long as they wish in order to help others. This may be done by conducting classes for those who desire to learn, by doing what might be likened to social work among the unenlightened spirits, maybe helping to raise those who died in childhood, or perhaps making efforts to contact Earth people to give them information about conditions beyond the grave.

A discarnate intelligence who has attained advancement may also go immediately to the next plane beyond, where he refines himself until a condition is reached in which he never, for even an instant, allows a thought to cross his mind that is not loving, compassionate and peaceful. He will then continue his joyous journey from plane to plane until he reaches, after unimaginable spiritual development, the ultimate plane of existence, which is perfection, and God.

So it is true that consciousness is in a state of evolution, and it eventually achieves union with the highest, but only after an advanced stage of development has been achieved, so the importance of knowing the necessity to mature your character on Earth cannot be overestimated. Otherwise, hundreds of years may be wasted as an ignorant soul flounders in a morass of despair or hatred, or an opinionated spirit hangs onto his old beliefs.

I must repeat once again: it is essential to progress as much as possible before you die. You do have free will and you must give more than lip service to your philosophy or religion, acting on its precepts in an attempt to improve yourself. Unless you have a good start on Earth, your advancement will be impeded after death, until you finally become aware of the magnificent destiny that awaits you.

TWENTY

TEACHING THE EARTHBOUND SPIRITS

When we were putting the finishing touches on Mother's chapter, we began to have an influx of intruders who ultimately caused us no end of trouble. There were weeks when Mother's power to write was so counteracted that she was unable to send more than an occasional brief message, and my hands were actually pulled from the typewriter whenever they were laid loosely on the keys hoping for contact. When I wrote for myself under my own steam, there were no problems, but my *relaxed* hands were never allowed to remain on the keys.

Harvey had made it clear to me that mischief-makers could be obnoxious. Still, it was difficult to believe that they were the cause of physical manifestations. I tried to find every possible normal excuse for it; to this modern woman, anything was preferable to believing in evil spirits—even when her typewriter was acting possessed.

It was disconcerting and, yes, frightening, to feel my fingers raised from the keys by a force I could not fathom. When I believed it was Mother communicating, I did not mind having my hands moved without my conscious effort. But this was altogether different. It seemed abnormal, chilling, as though something diabolical were taking hold of me.

Mother, with her understanding of ultimates, was not alarmed, and her refusal to worry, when she could get in a word to reassure me, would calm me somewhat, until the next time my efforts to write were rejected.

Soon the intruders began to dash off little messages to me—although they seemed to do it unwillingly—which revealed them to be human, at least, even though it did not explain why they were there. This writing began as a cold "Yes" that typed itself when I sat down to contact Mother. It was repellent to find this on my paper instead of Mother's cheery, "Good morning, Susy, dear" or "Let's go, honey."

If I persisted, trying to learn more about what was going on, the intruders might come out with, "You are not to write with your mother." Then they'd stop and nothing more would be written and my hands would be removed. An occasional "guard" would add a few words more. One was quite garrulous:

> I will not tell you anything. They forbid me to talk to you. This is wrong. I mean wrong for me to be typing. It is wrong for you to make any contact with me. You are not to do so. I do not wish to type with you. It is I who pull your fingers from the keys because I am not allowed to let you write to anyone. It is definitely prohibited. I must not write to you.

When asked who made such rules, they did not say. One was vehement in his assertions, and wrote:

> It is no use trying. You won't ever again be allowed to talk to anyone with a typewriter or pencil, so there's no use trying.

Once, for a day or two, the guard was either foreign or an ignoramus. He expressed himself thus: "This not mother. This man want you not write book."

Mother, when she could get a word in, insisted the guards were just the misguided spirits of those who needed help to learn the truth about their condition. She always got back to that. I must never think there were actual "evil spir-its" or "devils" causing the harm—they were only unenlight-ened invisible people.

When I began to realize that, I set to work to reform them and had good results. I began to read Mother's chapter aloud to them, and they listened. It clarified things they had-n't understood before. The first evidence of this occurred one night when the long-suffering Smith-Corona typed:

"Mother is not here. It is not Mother."

"Who is writing?" I asked.

"It is not anyone you know. It is someone who is not sup-posed to be a friend, but I must talk to you. Why is progres-sion so important? I wish I might discuss it further with you."

I immediately began reading the chapter aloud, and the next day the typewriter had a new guard, for overnight the previous one had started his upward journey. I could tell it was somebody new because the same old routine was started, fingers pulled off keys, and then finally words typed: "No, you can't write." After a day or two, this one also began to ask questions.

Frankly, I was much inclined to doubt the genuineness of these conversions. It seemed too easy. I found it hard to believe that a few words from me could make such a quick change in anyone. When Mother got the chance to explain it, she said:

> The truth is that because they can see you in a physical body and hear actual words come from your mouth addressed to them, they will listen to you. They hear nothing from you they have not already heard countless times since their deaths from the spirit helpers, but they pay attention because it comes from the familiar Earth surroundings instead of the new and strange. The moment a spirit understands his situation and expresses a desire to advance, his progression starts.

As our conversations became more frequent, the interruptions lessened, and soon the Smiths were having their good old typewritten chats again. Then I unburdened to Bill Hanemann the problem of the interference we'd had. While it was at its worst I did not dare talk about it for fear he'd misunderstand, but when it was behind me it didn't matter.

At first Bill peered at me for symptoms of hysteria. Satisfied that I had myself under reasonable control, he then began insisting that Mother be questioned to find out just what the hell was going on in a universe where malevolent characters were allowed to run around undisciplined, pulling people's fingers off keys.

Mother's attempts to explain stressed her point that each individual must learn self-discipline:

> You should not forget that everyone arrives here in the same mental state in which he lived, for no one's mind is any different immediately after death than it was the moment before. If he was a delinquent or a man with a bitter or corrupt nature, that is what he remains. It is the opinionated person whose mind is closed to new ideas who has the hardest time. He resists all new concepts, rejecting everything he doesn't understand. On Earth, no one could tell him anything; in this plane, no one can tell him anything either.

Mother said that an unenlightened newcomer in the spirit world is in more or less of a fog, which continues until his perception is cleared by the development of his understanding. He sees only what he concentrates on, and that is most likely to be the place where he died and the people, or type of people, with whom he had passed most of his time. He may spend many years wandering around in his own personal miasma, trying to stay as close as possible to the Earth life he previously knew. To be told that by his own thinking he makes the conditions in which he exists means nothing to him, and he becomes inured to conversation about it.

"I can't see why he wouldn't listen and give it a try," I commented.

"Some do. More don't. It's exactly as you yourself wear mental earplugs against the exhortations of the radio to buy this and buy that," Mother answered.

"Well, if there is an audience, no matter how invisible, I'll lecture every day."

"I'm glad," Mother told me. "I hope you always will try to get the truth to them. There are so many who must be taught, and as I said, they will listen to you. Since there's no way to discipline these Earthbound spirits who are troublesome, it's only possible to aid them by converting them one at a time to their need to improve themselves. And no matter how deep their degradation, some day someone will get through to each of them with the truth. It is inevitable."

"But pulling fingers off typewriter keys seems like awfully silly work for spooks, who could be using their time and talents to haunt houses." I still couldn't see why they bothered with me.

Mother said it was because I was dabbling in their sphere of action. Anyone who tries to communicate is to some extent putting himself at their mercy.

"Everyone who dies rebellious is a potential source of mischief," she wrote. "If they knew all that I've been telling you before they died, they wouldn't be unhappy souls in the Hereafter with nothing better to do than play pranks or make trouble."

"If we hadn't personally put up with Harvey and these other juvenile delinquents, I'd think you were out of your ever-lovin' mind," I said. "Real live dead people invisibly wafting about in the air heckling us communicators—honestly!"

"You don't hear me arguing," Mother replied. "I'd never have believed it myself until I got here."

Very shortly I had more evidence that she was right. Once, late in the spring after Harvey had been in limbo for several months, I was sitting outdoors in the sun, proofreading copy. I needed a comment from Mother about something she had written the night before, so I picked up my pencil and held it for her to write.

What was produced instead was "I love you, Harvey."

I shrieked, "Oh, no, not you again!" It had been so long since Harvey had troubled me that I presumed he'd gone away. "Where've you been?" I asked him. I could almost hear his plaintive whine as he wrote, "I can't type." Asked why he continued to hang around when he couldn't communicate with me anymore, he wrote that he'd been learning a lot. When he'd had to stop pestering me because Mother and I were using the typewriter, he was furious, but then he began to listen to what we were discussing about progression. He heard so much about the opportunities for advancement for a young spirit willing to travel that he became interested. Now he was almost bursting to tell me of his eagerness to start his progression.

Mother and the other spirit helpers around gave him the answers to his questions—things they'd tried to tell him before when he was so contrary he wouldn't listen—and now he responded eagerly. He apologized for all the trouble he'd caused me, stayed around a few days longer, and then suddenly he disappeared, never to return.

Remember when Grandpa Anderson told me several months earlier that the only way to get rid of Harvey was to cease writing to him and to teach him? Thus the little moral to Harvey's story seems to be that Mother and her grandfather knew what they were talking about when they wrote: "The only way to eliminate evil is to convert it to good."

From time to time, Mother continued briefing me about this life and the next:

> Natural laws govern everything on Earth and in each plane of existence. Every person lives his life within these laws, and only when they are observed is he

successful. There is never an instance when natural laws are set aside or broken to help either a person on Earth or a spirit on any other plane. If it seems that there is, it is only because of your limited understanding of these laws. What seem to be miracles are only the operation of lesser-known laws.

It makes life intelligible and purposeful to know that we live in a planned universe where system predominates. We so often tend to attribute things to blind chance. But no, Mother told me, according to plan each man lives his life on Earth to learn from his experiences and from his daily contacts with other people, then he continues in the etheric to gain more knowledge until he has advanced enough that he may progress to other planes. This design is the same for each man and woman who lives, there being no individual arrangements, no special privileges, no divine dispensations for anyone.

"Hard luck can be endured with more fortitude when one realizes the instruction he can get from the unfortunate situation," Mother said, adding that then the same lesson won't have to be mastered in some more difficult manner later:

> There is no person who escapes any of life's lessons, and if it seems that a benevolent providence protects some and not others, that is only a misconception, for character is at no time achieved without toil. If one's life has been so effortless on Earth that he has acquired no wisdom, then it will be necessarily more difficult for him on the next plane.

"All this sounds to me like cause and effect," I commented.

> It is, exactly. The effect doesn't always occur to the one who caused it to happen, but it is still a result of

the act. And one who makes a careless mistake or does a malicious deed on Earth must rectify it to the best of his ability or else he will have to make recompense in the etheric.

I was startled. "You mean there's an accountant who keeps records of each person's life?"

No, there is no one whose duty it is to keep tab on each man. He does it himself. All his memories are available to him after death; and when a spirit begins to progress, it is his own decision what he shall make requital for and how he will go about it. If each man on Earth knew that his own progress is dependent upon himself alone, he would be more eager to begin his forward growth before he dies.

"You and your reactionary theories," I said. "Cause and effect . . . free will . . . self-discipline. The behaviorists would be after your head."

I can't help it. These terms are all valid. Just because concepts are old is no reason to reject them. But then, just because a belief has been prevalent for a long time is no reason to accept it, either. Man has had many glimpses of the truth in the past and he'll have many more before he ever gets the whole picture. But eventually every child will be raised knowing how to think properly to bring out his finest capabilities.

"That'll be the day," I said skeptically, musing about human nature, another of the old saws Mother was apparently overlooking.

Yes, I'm an idealist. We all are here where I am. But we have the advantage of knowing the overall long-range

plan or scheme of the universe. It is good, believe me;
it is *good*.

We had a visitor shortly thereafter who told us from his
own experience about the processes of learning he had been
going through on the first plane of existence and even
beyond. One night Mother paused in her typing, and at that
moment, I had a sudden feeling of my father's presence that
was overpoweringly strong. Then Mother typed, "Your
Daddy's here."

Goose bumps popped out all over me and I said, "Put
him on, quick," and then he typed with me. After greetings,
he identified himself with personal information such as his
middle name—a great secret because he disliked it—and then
went on, that night and the next day, to write several pages to
me. I was so elated I could hardly keep my fingers going, yet
eagerly let him type in order to learn what he wanted to tell
me. The most encouraging part of it was his praise of me:

> I'll never know how you have managed to develop
> into such a sweet person all alone in the world for so
> long as you have been. Your Mother has been gone
> seven years. During that time you have been alone
> most of the time trying to make your way in the world
> . . . and with a handicap, too. But out of it has come
> this lovely, lovely person.

At this point, I came right out and stated that this was
obviously wishful thinking on my part; that my subconscious
mind was certainly feeding me what I most wanted to hear.

> There is no subconscious mind involved here; it is
> your own father who comes back to Earth from anoth-
> er plane of existence and finds a daughter of whom he
> can be very proud.

Daddy explained that he had worked extremely hard on his progression during the nearly twenty-five years since he left us, and that after Mother joined him, he had been ready to advance, so he went on to the next plane. He tried to make me aware that he lives in a condition of serenity in which he always thinks thoughts of love and is never negative about anything, and yet life isn't dull for him. This last was in answer to the question I knew Bill Hanemann would inevitably put when told about this. Daddy said he is surrounded by fascinating people who are busy doing interesting and enjoyable things. It sounded to me as if he had already landed in paradise, but he said he has a tremendous way to go yet before he reaches the heights.

TWENTY-ONE

MORE SPOOKS—AND THEY TALK DIRTY

When I offer the assurance that this chapter does not report a hysterical interlude, I hope it is believed. When I wrote *Confessions of a Psychic*, I felt that if by publishing it I could keep even a few persons who hear voices they can't account for out of institutions and help them learn how to cope with the situation, my torment wouldn't have been in vain. Unfortunately, too many people get into similar situations because of their ignorance of the dangers of attempting spirit communication without proper protection.

Because my adventures were what might be considered "mental," there is the possibility that a critic would be sure it was a psychotic episode. I must declare, however, that during the entire time these disturbances were going on I felt exactly as sane and sensible as at this moment—if anyone can ever be sure he is entirely sane and sensible. My mental state would have been similar on any ordinary day of my life under any normal circumstances if at the same time I was bedeviled by a plague of mosquitoes, or if there was an incessant ringing of my telephone. It was irritating and tiring, and it even became frightening, but my own mind, the thinking part of me, was existing aside from these activities, observing what was going on at all times.

People all over the world—educated, reasonable types who might get together for any kind of study group—sit to develop their psychic abilities. They have discovered that they have some type of psychic sensitivity, and they get together at regular intervals to improve it. They feel an obligation to become as proficient as possible—just as one might who discovered an aptitude for music or art. Some of these persons have a talent for telepathy—they can give occasional accurate reports of what others are thinking. Some are clairvoyant and see pictures or lights and colors that the rest of the group are unable to see. Some, who are clairaudient, hear voices that are inaudible to others. Some are aware of words spoken independently within their minds—this is clairsentience. For those who develop these gifts under guidance from mediums or others who have already grown in psychical talents, everything proceeds satisfactorily, because they are all perfectly normal types of mediumship through which evidential information is frequently produced.

My problem was that I got into a clairsentient phase without knowing anything about it. It came on too suddenly and without proper preparation. At the time, I was acquainted with no one who had ever been through anything similar so that he could give me advice; and I had no idea what to do to overcome it. It was the most unnerving experience of my life.

Just after I awoke on the morning of June 2, singing in my mind were the words, "Happy birthday to you, happy birthday to you." It seemed very chummy of me to sing to myself. I wondered why, if my subconscious was doing it, it wasn't singing my usual version—"Happy birthday to *me*." As the song progressed, it became clear that Mother was the one serenading. I thanked her and went about my business, unaware of what an unusual thing had actually occurred. It certainly was not evident to me that this was my first indication that a new psychic talent had developed.

The next evidence of it was revealed by my Aunt Ivy, who had been in the spirit world two years longer than Mother and had gone over with a long head start on her progression.

While on Earth, she had been the most Christlike human I had ever known, devoting her life totally to helping others. Now, in her invisible form, she had called on us several times during that spring in Daytona Beach. The first time she came, in March, my fingers were in position on the keys when suddenly I felt luminous, as though a bright shining light was pervading me, and I thought of my Aunt Ivy. Then Mother typed "My sister is here."

Aunt Ivy didn't try to type with me—she never was one for mechanical things—but Mother relayed on the typewriter a few exchanges from her, and this kind of sociable palaver went on after that whenever she dropped by.

On June 6, Mother typed that Aunt Ivy was there and that she wanted to try to communicate with me in my own mind. Always agreeable—beyond the point of questioning anything they might undertake; what could startle me now?—I tried to blank my mind in preparation for whatever might happen next. Then, spoken distinctly within my head, were the words "Aunt Ivy is talking to you, Susy Ethel." It was surprising after all, because she had never combined my two names before—nor had anyone else. Apparently this was her way of proving that it was she and not my own mind, which had tossed out "Ethel" long before.

I sang out happily that I could hear her, and she went on: "I was sure you were ready to try to communicate with us in this manner. I am beaming these words into your mind telepathically and you understand them."

As she slowly and distinctly impressed each thought upon me, it came to me exactly as though words were being spoken inside my head but not by me. My own ego or consciousness was intact, remaining quietly in a different spot in my head listening to what Aunt Ivy was saying. Also, the conversation was not anything I would have been likely to bring up. She talked mostly about her own son and daughter, with whom I had lost touch, and her eagerness to have them learn the truth about survival.

Then other words came, interrupting Aunt Ivy. "Let me try it, let me try it" . . . and there was Mother, eager to test this new mode of communication. She and I had a good time playing with it for nearly a week. My day began with "Good morning, Mother" spoken aloud and her reply in my mind. We continued this way all through the day, even to her "I'd iron the sleeves first if I were you" and "Don't put that egg there, you'll knock it off."

Yes, she bossed me just as she always had all my life, but now it didn't bother me. I'd proved myself able to live without her guidance, so now was able to take it in the spirit it was intended without getting my back up.

It was all great fun at first, but then something different happened. *Everybody* tried to get into the act. Other entities who heard us talking learned Mother's technique and took over. The Baddies muscled in on our new diversion and spoiled it as they did everything else. For three days and nights I was heckled constantly by mental conversation from outsiders who had no right to intrude. For the rest of that year, they bothered me on occasion until I learned how to close my mind to them entirely—even though it also meant closing out those who had a legitimate right to talk to me.

"Can you become insane on just one subject and still be normal in every other way?" I wondered. I had not lost touch with reality, but my demons began to try to make me think so. The invisible hoods who heard my question answered with, "Yes, you're going crazy; you're definitely losing your mind. We'll drive you crazy." This went on inside my head all day long.

At first I panicked. "If I haven't already cracked up, I certainly will if this keeps up. Positive thoughts! Mother's good old standby . . . try them." So, I'd give myself a pep talk: "You're not a sissy, Susy. You've overcome all the other things that have come up in your life and you'll beat this."

Then the intruders took up that refrain: "Susy's a sissy; Susy's a sissy." They interspersed that with their, "You're going crazy; we're driving you crazy."

The first night they almost got me. I called for help from everybody I knew in the spirit world: Mother, Daddy, Aunt Ivy, Nina (wherever she was), Grandpa Anderson—anyone but Harvey! Trying to sleep and being unable to have a moment's peace because of the constantly reiterated "You're going crazy. You're a sissy and you're going crazy," I got out of bed time after time to read, having discovered that the only way to shut them out was to keep my mind so occupied with something else that I couldn't pay attention to them. But whenever drowsiness would overcome me and I'd retire again, the refrain would resume. I don't know why it didn't occur to me then to try to convert them, as I had done with the typewriter guards; but this was somehow so different and so much more appalling that it hardly seemed as if it could be coming from anything human. I was just too involved at first to even think of reading Mother's chapter to them.

It did occur to me that praying might be a good idea. I still wasn't sure about any kind of a God who might be interested in paying personal attention to me, but I was now willing to try to find out. So, standing up in the middle of the floor of the trailer, I dared the unknown to harm me, saying firmly, "I have help greater than any of you and I know how to reach it." Then I hurled out into the great expanse of spirit, clear out to this new concept of God that Mother had presented to me (but which I was not yet aware was *within* me as well), a powerful prayer for assistance.

In a few moments a gentle voice spoke to me, inside my mind, of course, like all the others. But he sounded kindly.

"Your rescuer has arrived," he said. "I have come from a far plane to take care of you. You will have no more trouble." He was convincing, and he stopped the others from talking.

"Thank you, God," I said, relaxing in the peace that ensued, slipping back into bed as if into my new friend's sheltering arms.

"There now, rest," he said, "you're safe now. Just relax." I projected my thoughts toward him, reaching, yearning for his reassurance.

"Come to me, come to me, Susy," he lulled me. "I can protect you."

This was so great that I rested, soothed and comfortable for the first time all day.

"Come to me," he went on, slowly and softly, "leave your body . . . slip right out of your body and come to me."

A cold, hard lump dropped to the pit of my stomach and I started up quickly to complete alertness and terror. His suggestions reminded me of everything I had read about the possible dangers of out-of-body experiences. Sometimes, it is said, one's consciousness might leave the body and be unable to return because a spirit entity jumps in and possesses it while it is unoccupied. His idea was against all Mother's teachings, and I realized it in time to reject him.

"You're not trying to help me! You're evil!" I shouted, leaping out of bed as if to run away from him.

How he laughed! "I almost had you," he gloated. "One more minute and you'd have come soaring right out to me. Then you'd never have been able to get back into your body."

"Go away!" I was shaking all over by then. "You can't harm me. I have protection, lots of it. Leave me alone! Mother, Daddy, help me, please!"

"Oh, I'll get you; never fear. I'll either kill you or drive you insane. You'll never publish that book."

I went outside and walked up and down the road, afraid to go back into the trailer until the sky began to hint that the safety of daylight was approaching. Then sleep finally came.

My antagonist was there the next morning as soon as I awoke, trying to kill me as he had promised. He was sending some kind of electric shocks constantly through my body. These were different from nervousness or tension, although naturally I suspected those at first. Completely debilitating and shattering, they attacked my bowels and weakened my whole system.

On top of that, he was talking to me in the dirtiest words he could say. All that day spoken into my mind were four-letter words that I never used. This was before the era when such words became commonplace, popping up in almost anything you read, and they were revolting to me. My discomfiture only made the entity continue. I had a day of this, with only one slight advantage—if you can call it that: by evening my body was so exhausted by the attack that I dropped off to sleep right away.

I did not know it then, having never read about such things, but this profanity deal is standard operating procedure for malevolent communicators. As far as the physical shocks are concerned, I have never heard of that particular treatment being given to anyone else, but much other unpleasantness occurs, frequently involving sexual urges. Fortunately I was spared that.

The third morning my invisible enemy started with the same routine, apparently determined either to kill me with his etheric shocks or else bore me to death with filth, but that day I found the way to finish him off. On one particular occasion he tried to use a vulgar phrase that I didn't know, and he couldn't get it into my mind. Realizing what he was trying to do and how he was innocently being blocked, I laughed, then taunted him about it. He retaliated by sending more bolts of his enervating lightning through my system while repeating viciously, "I'm going to kill you. I'll *kill* you!" I almost thought he was succeeding.

I'd finally discovered his secret weakness, however. He could be made fun of. If I couldn't beat him, I'd join him and rib him to distraction.

"All right, Sam, you son of a bitch," I said. "I've been around, too, you know. Just because I don't use dirty words is no sign I don't know at least some of them." Then I said a few choice epithets to show him. After that, whenever he spoke profanity in my mind I matched him aloud with some of my own. And I addressed him as Sam every time.

Then it wasn't a fight anymore. My intruder degenerated from a fiend of magnitude coming from outer space to do me great harm into a petulant, invisible derelict who didn't like being referred to snidely by a name that wasn't his own and didn't want to be laughed at. He particularly could not understand my mirth. He began to talk to me about it.

"How can you laugh at me?" he asked. "Why don't you hate me? I'm really trying to kill you." He wanted me to hate him because violent emotion challenged him. My lack of rancor toward him, after all his meanness, was incomprehensible to him.

"I can see into your mind," he said, "and I don't see hatred for anyone. It isn't just me alone. You really don't hate anybody. I don't understand you." This was extremely encouraging. I was glad to know the results of my year's efforts at self-improvement were so obvious.

"My mother insists on the importance of loving my fellow man," I explained. "You probably have to be considered in that category, however weird you are." I told him it wasn't actually possible to love anyone as misguided as he, but compassion was the next best thing, and that I had sympathy for him as well because he was so ignorant of his true situation. This cued me straight to Mother's chapter and he seemed to go along willingly, apparently listening as I read it aloud.

When I was through he said, "So that's why some of these goofy guys around me are always insisting they can see people and lights and hear all kinds of music that I can't." Then he thanked me and left me alone for the rest of the day. The next morning, he was apparently gone, but unfortunately, there were new voices to contend with, calling in my mind, "Can you hear me? Can you hear me? I'm going to kill you or drive you crazy."

"Oh, no, you're not," I said immediately. "I'm going to convert you instead." Short work was made of each new entity, but it was still a darned nuisance. I couldn't get any work done for reading that chapter aloud all the time. I didn't appreciate the idea that my mind was open and vulnerable to the likes of them, anyway. Even if they had become removable, I didn't feel up to handling a new batch of trouble like that every day. I had to learn how to keep them out in the first place.

My own guides hadn't actually seemed to be of much assistance. Where else could I turn? To a spiritualist minister, obviously. I returned to the medium who had tried to help me rid myself of Harvey, even though her Indians hadn't known as much about spirit psychology as Grandpa had. She told me a sure cure for my problems was to dip my hands and arms into water up to the elbows and instead of drying them, fling the water from them. At the same time I would fling away all evil spirits, she said.

I was desperate enough to try that, but with no results, unfortunately. The entities who were intruding themselves on my thoughts just laughed at me until I read them Mother's chapter.

This medium also said that if the water-flinging didn't do the trick, I should stand barefoot outside on the ground with my back against a tree, for trees have great life force and I could absorb power from the Earth through my feet. It seemed only slightly more sensible than flinging water from my elbows, but I gave it a trial, too. In fact, several nights during the summer when I couldn't sleep because of being tormented by unseen talkers, I'd slip outside in my nightie and robe and bare feet and lean against the rough hide of the big palm tree out front and ask it to share its strength with me (but not its palmetto bugs). Getting outside away from the increasing oppressiveness of the trailer was good, for at least I was cooled off by the freshness of the night air.

Bill Hanemann was finally burdened with my problem because I had to talk to *someone* about the voices. He knew the oft prophesied hysteria had finally arrived, even though his prying scrutiny could reveal no traces of it in the rest of my thinking or reactions. Determined to keep me grounded, he insisted I give up all efforts at communication immediately. Dr. Hornell Hart, appealed to at Duke, advised the same thing.

Of course, my parents had been implored for help constantly all during this time. "Get me some Indians!" I'd demanded. Everyone who believed in spirits believed that Indians had more power to protect you from the boogies than anyone else. So, "Get me some Indians," I pleaded, "a whole tribe, big and brawny with etheric power. Send for help, Mother, for God's sake. Get me some Indians!"

Do you know what Mother said in return (the few times she could write anything to me in spite of the interference)? Still promoting Grandpa's theory that the only way to get rid of them was to convert them, she agreed with Hornell and Bill that my best bet was to stop any efforts at communication until this thing blew over. I thought she was much too calm about it.

I told Bill my situation was exactly like a man treading water in the middle of the ocean. It was easy enough for everyone to shout advice to him to get back to the shore. But how could he take it? The only raft they threw him was a warning to ignore the water. It was enough for them to talk. I was the one breasting the bounding billows, still treading water with all my might. Every time my mind lay idle for a second someone was communicating with *me*. I wasn't the one communicating. I was being communicated to. Stop treading water, they said. Rush back to shore, they said. Don't talk to them, they said. Ha!

Or, to use another metaphor, let go of the tail of the lion who's chewing on your big toe.

It was reassuring eventually to learn that Daddy and Aunt Ivy had been there rendering aid. Apparently, however, they weren't doing anything except talking to the interlopers and rounding up other bands of spirit missionaries to talk to them. This supplemented the daily "sermons" I gave to those who pestered me. And gradually these villains, too, began to be less obnoxious and to become aware of themselves as something better than pests. The vocal persecution was eventually to let up, just as the pulling-fingers-off-keys had eased.

But I seldom dared to take a chance to instigate any communication.

I did not stop working on my book, even though it was obviously unwise to appeal to Mother for help on it. My life was so involved with it that there was nothing else in the world I wanted to do but keep at it.

It was the hottest summer imaginable. In an uninsulated trailer in steamy Florida, I sat under an electric fan every minute, wore the skimpiest costumes legal, and perspired constantly. I had to make a conscious effort at all times to keep my mind closed against the voices. Whenever they'd bother me I'd start singing a song, paying careful attention to my articulation of each word, or reading a detective story or some other book that would grip my interest at once, when I wasn't reading Mother's chapter aloud. I had to keep my mind occupied constantly.

As I remained on constant red alert, I thought, "Look at all that has happened to me just because of picking up a Ouija board without knowing what I was doing." No wonder Mother was so set against naively fooling around with spirit communication, even when she was so eager for me to accomplish something with it.

Years later a dear friend, Clarissa Mulders, who has since gone over to the other side herself, fussed at me a lot. In fact, she was always nagging at me about my rigidity. She said, "Susy, why do you insist that I must not try to use Ouija? Give me the privilege to make mistakes if I want to. I'd rather take my own chances of getting into trouble, even if the same thing might happen to me that happened to you."

If you see someone else, especially someone you love, starting to jump into a whirlpool bath of boiling water in which you have just been almost scalded, you can't help but warn her against it. It could be that many persons have been in that same water under different circumstances and merely had a pleasant warm bath. Still, the fact that on numerous unpredictable occasions the thermostat went out of control and the temperature became so hot as to be dangerous should cause people to avoid it altogether. At least, that's the way I see it, and that's why I am adamant that you not make any attempt at spirit communication without protecting yourself thoroughly and learning the proper techniques.

While I was going through the worst of it, I had a different attitude. I knew that our mental processes are so terribly complicated that we haven't even begun to understand them, that there are more miles of unexplored territory in the human cortex than there are in Brazil, and that there was the possibility that my entire experience with the voices was subjective, because hallucinations always seem real to the person who has them. But my friends attested that except for this slight tendency to hear voices inside my head, I was in just as good shape as anybody. That was slightly encouraging.

TWENTY-TWO

GETTING GUIDES FOR PROTECTION—OR NOT

In early October, for the first time since my return to Daytona, I called Minnie's Beauty Shop for an appointment to get my tousled topknot professionally groomed. It was surprising to have such a strong compulsion to tell my old friend, Minnie, about my interest in psychical research, but as soon as I sat down in her chair, a recital of my current interests began. (As you become more and more sensitive you seem to know instinctively to whom you can safely talk about this subject.) Well, all the while she was doing my hair, Minnie was besting my stories, for she had personally seen apparitions of her grandmother and her father-in-law. I had nothing to offer as sensational as that.

I told her of my need to develop my incipient mediumship to the point where controls and guides who could protect me would always be there. My beautician had a suggestion for me. Another customer of hers—Emmaline Gerts, we'll call her—was a nonprofessional medium who had said she would like to have someone attend development classes with her. It is through such sittings that one's psychic abilities can grow, so this might fill my need exactly. Minnie felt confident of the integrity of this woman, whom she had known for years. I called her on returning home and made an appointment for that Saturday night.

On my arrival, tall, heavyset Gerts immediately took me to the basement of her home where she had a séance room, with dark curtains over all the windows so that it was possible to black it out completely. She put me in a chair across a table from her and turned out all the lights. There we sat in a pool of ink.

The dark had never done anything particularly reassuring for me (although I've since learned to rather enjoy sitting with development groups in darkened rooms), and being in it alone with this sizeable seer was disconcerting. I didn't know for sure what mediums did when you were alone with them in the dark. It was doubtful that she personally might be interested, say, in swinging a chair at me, but who knew what notions would occur to some entity that might possess her?

Just then she set up a loud snorting and sputtering, and a noisy etheric character named Dr. Sommers started shouting at the top of Gerts's lungs. But his message was friendly even if his audio control left something to be desired. He gave a dissertation of welcome, assuring me of his active interest in my welfare.

The medium, who had remained conscious while her vocal apparatus was borrowed by Dr. Sommers, thanked him for coming, and then began describing lights that she could see all around me. She said they were the emanations of benevolent spirits.

"They're *very* welcome," I said, in my eagerness indicating for the first time the possibility of any urgent need on my part. Gerts had been told nothing about me except my desire to sit for development.

"Hey, there, you with the yellow light," Gerts vigorously addressed the blackness around her. "Who are you? What's your name? Shine up your star there, boy. Speak up. Oh, Yellow Fox, is it? Are you her guide? Speak louder so I can hear you. What? What?"

Then she relayed the information that Yellow Fox was an Indian who was now mine, all mine. During the evening she also discovered the brilliantly glowing light of a young Indian girl who was going to stay with me too. She expected to be my control when I developed my mediumship.

Now we were getting somewhere. The acquisition of a sufficient number of Indian chums might let me get back into active contact with Mother again.

"Wonder if they're Comanches or Iroquois or Sioux," I mused while sitting there quietly in the dark. "A gal named Susy really should have a Sioux Indian as her . . . "

"Who's that?" roared Gerts, and I jumped two feet, seven inches into the air. She then described a beautiful violet light beside me.

"How wonderful for you," she said, seeming almost envious. "You have a great teacher here, an Oriental gentleman." She told me his name was something like Solas—I'm not broadcasting the true names given me for my guides; it is not considered to be in good taste. "He and the Indians have been with you for the past month. They will stay. Your family on the other side has been instrumental in securing this group of spirits to protect you."

"He's welcome," I greeted him, impressed at the magnitude of my new coterie. "They all are."

"Solas is bearded and wears a strange type of turban," Gerts added. "I can't exactly place it . . . I think it's Persian or Turkish or something like that. Yes, he tells me it is Persian."

We sat a while longer in the dark, but nothing new developed, and then I went home, not as encouraged as one might think. Parapsychologists would have scoffed at this Indian powwow, and hence so must I, for she really hadn't given me anything evidential that couldn't have come from her imagination. I was much inclined to dismiss her and the three spirit strangers she'd introduced me to, feeling that another door had been closed in my face.

All the next day I took stock of myself, rather dispiritedly. Without Mother to answer questions for me, nothing more could be done on the enlightening aspects of my book, and I'd brought the narrative portion of it up to date. I was in the doldrums, not knowing what to do with myself. Maybe I needed to get into something creative with my hands again, but what? The trailer didn't need painting. What other big project could I start? Well, it would soon be close to Christmas, so maybe I could make my greeting cards. Let's see . . . How could I assure them to be indigenously Floridian? Seashells, of course; shell poinsettias glued on my cards. Why, come to think of it, they gave courses in jewelry making at some of the shell shops, I could learn to make my own Christmas presents. So there I was, enthusiastic again, with a project ahead of me.

Early Monday morning, I trekked across town to a shop where this Florida specialty (jewelry intricately designed from dyed shells) is made and sold. I joined a class and sat for several hours awkwardly manipulating with tweezers tiny pikakas and gars and other shells with funny names. At Christmas there was big business in shell jewelry, and I learned to take leaf- or petal-shaped or coiled seashells that had been dyed red or green and glue them into pins and earrings. When decorated with pearls and sequins, they were quite attractive.

Once, leaning back for a rest, I let my eyes wander around the room and noticed an Aquarian Bible among some books on a shelf. I mentioned it because it is read by many metaphysicians, and learned that Lois, the instructor and owner of the shop, was a newly ordained minister in the spiritualist church. After the lesson, I waited to talk to her, asking her if she had a circle that sat regularly for development.

"Sit by yourself," Lois said in her abrupt manner. "You can develop mediumship that way. I did."

"I'm afraid to," I told her. "I have intruders who try to talk to me much of the time. What I need is protection."

This woman intimated that I was a softy to want any more spirit guides and protectors than were already with me.

"But I don't have any!"

"You do, too. You have two Indians and a Master from the East right here with you now. What more do you need?"

"Really?" I was alerted quickly. "Tell me more."

Lois peered somewhere back of my left ear, as if sizing up this contingent she saw there. "One of the Indians is a big brave and the other is a young girl—I'd say in her middle teens. The older man, the Master, wears an Oriental turban of some kind. He has a beard."

I was delighted at this independent confirmation of what Gerts had told me. Having already learned that a medium could take whatever you revealed and make something of it, I had said nothing personal to either of them and deliberately had not spoken to Lois of what Gerts had produced. Also, I had not taken it seriously enough to bother repeating it.

These women had not given me anything routine, either. An Indian brave and a young Indian girl and an Asian gentleman are not necessarily the usual familiars of one developing psychic sensitivity. It could as easily have been three braves and five squaws, or Mommy and Daddy, or Aunt Violet and Uncle Harry, or any other combination.

The mediums, not knowing each other and living in opposite ends of town, could not have gotten together and made up the story to tell me. Lois had not even known I was coming until her opening door revealed my countenance. On knowing them better, I came to realize that both women were scornful of subterfuge, and were strictly lone wolves, attending to their own business. Yet both had given me identical information in almost identical language.

Unless telepathy is so highly involved that the second medium read from my mind thoughts the first one had implanted and that I had rejected and was not at the moment recalling, then something interesting had been presented to me. I have heard no evidence of any sort that telepathy works in such a convoluted fashion.

For the first time I began to take the Indians seriously. I went back to Gerts after that and sat regularly with her for development every Saturday night for twelve weeks. During that time nothing ever happened of an evidential nature, but my group of spirit associates was enlarged and my contact with them strengthened.

Evidence is the most important thing in psychical research. Mediums always try to bring information that can be identified by the sitter. I had learned at Duke that nothing involving spirit communication is any good without proof. Precognition is valuable too. Mediums try to tell you something that will come true, and some of the better historical mediums, like Leonard, Piper, and Garret, produced some doozies. (That is, Gladys Osborne Leonard, Lenore Piper and Eileen Garrett, tops in their profession during their lifetimes.)

All those who form my protective band were said to be doing this Good Samaritan stint as part of their own spiritual progression. Throughout our relationship, each has played his own individual role, and although I have never been able to learn much about them personally, each has always seemed to stay in character. I am sure they have done what they could to protect me, but it took much more cooperation on my part than I first realized. I don't think they were aware then, either, that bodily defense would be needed as well as mental. But on December 4, they were suddenly alerted to twenty-four-hour sentry duty.

That day, tripping over a small dog that came to play with Junior and got himself tangled in my feet. I landed solidly on the ground with my arm against a brick bordering the flower bed and broke my right wrist in two places.

I hardly dare claim specifically that a rascally influence upended me, or that it caused any of the other accidents that began to happen to me consistently for a period of time, but I'd lived for many years without breaking anything more important than an occasional dish or breakfast egg. I even managed to slide through ten winters on the icy hills of Western Maryland and successfully evade a spill. Now I was finally brought down by a sun-kissed Florida puppy, and from then on—for over six months—the accidents kept happening.

My guides, apparently napping until the moment my wrist cracked, jumped into action, I presumed to make things as easy as possible for me. But why did they let it happen in the first place? I was somewhat miffed. Still, after its initial intensity, the pain was always bearable and I was calm. So calm, in fact, that I had a terrible time convincing any of my neighbors that my arm was broken so that someone would take me to the doctor.

After I finally got to the emergency room, though, and returned home with my arm in a cast, Irene, Nan, Rena, and Bill and Helen Hanemann were mobilized. All kinds of wonderful service was available from then on.

It wasn't too unpleasant, actually, living alone with a broken wing, except that Junior didn't understand. He demanded his customary attention, including his usual number of walks around the block every day, even though I hadn't promenaded without my cane for fifteen years and found it exhausting. Cooking wasn't a problem at first because Irene showed up the next day with a huge pot of stew so I wouldn't have to think about what to eat for a week. There was such a great quantity of it that I rarely thought about eating stew for years afterward.

I did feel mistreated a few days later when I tripped while trying to negotiate the step into the trailer and gashed my shin on the sharp metal doorsill. This time I gave a yelp of pain, afraid my leg was broken, too. That would have been almost too much. Where were those darned guides? They were hardly earning their keep, the way I saw it.

But everything came out all right eventually. The arm was out of the cast in ten weeks, numb for over six months because of using the walking stick too soon, and then entirely well, and that was the end of that.

Except for one little thing. Several weeks after the cast was removed I accompanied a friend to a crowded Sunday afternoon session at nearby Cassadaga Spiritualist Camp, where a visiting medium from New York was to give messages.

The question I wrote on my slip of paper (called a billet), which was put with all the others into a basket, was merely, "A message, please." I signed the initials, "S. S." on the outside of the folded sheet.

Later the basket was placed in front of the medium and she began to give readings. Eventually she picked up my billet and called out my initials across the large auditorium. When they were acknowledged, she asked, "Have you recently tripped over anything?"

"Yes," I answered.

"What was it?" she asked. "I'm just curious."

"A puppy."

As the audience laughed in sympathy, she added, "Well, I just wondered, for the message I get for you is this: 'Your tripping days are over. You will be taken care of.'"

A nice sentiment. I only wish it had been true.

TWENTY-THREE

JAMES ARRIVES, INCOGNITO

The muse becoming active again, a broken arm couldn't keep me from work, so right after the first of the year I was back at the typewriter, left-handed at first, but not for long. Fingers in a cast are supposed to be exercised, so I exercised them. I had to be sure my facts of etheric enlightenment were correct before daring to send my book to a publisher, so it seemed imperative to get my communication system reactivated. The talkers in my mind had stopped bothering me because I had kept myself closed to them for so long, and I made certain not to attempt any spoken communication with Mother again. But there seemed no reason we couldn't get together at the typewriter, and we did.

Very soon, though, Mother turned me over to a new scribe, who she said would help me with the philosophy because he would have more power to get through to me and he knew so much more than she did. My new communicant identified himself as James Anderson. When asked personal data about himself so that I could try to check if he was a benign individual or some intruder, or else a figment of my subconscious, he told me a few vague facts, but nothing iden-tifiable. He said he had died early in this century, that he had lived in Massachusetts, and that he'd had children. Nothing more specific could be learned from him.

As time went on, I came to suspect that "James Anderson" was a pseudonym for some well known person who was still active in trying to send enlightening data to the world, but for a long time no indication was given as to who it was—except that mediums wherever I went gave me the initials *W* or *J* or the names William or James. The few personal facts he gave me fit the biography of the famous Harvard psychologist and philosopher William James.

Eventually he told me that he was indeed this person, but he knew, and I admitted, that if he had come to me initially with a celebrated name, I would have thought him a phony. "Sir Oliver Lodge" of London once gave me some exacting information he said could be proved to provide evidence of his veracity, but after spending time and effort to check it, I learned it was untrue. In contrast, James and I have become very good friends and collaborators over the years, and he has written several books through me.

When he started communicating, the first subject James Anderson took up was the danger to beginners of taking the Ouija board seriously. He said it was even risky to play with it as a game because you might be taken in by it. He wrote that the spirit who claims to be the one you wish to contact may actually be an ill-natured interloper trying to make trouble or mischief. He entertainingly described the menace of the unseen. "It's as hazardous," he wrote, "as advertising in the newspaper for an honorably intentioned mate."

I agreed with him perfectly from my own experience with Harvey. When I said this, it was revealed that James knew nothing about Harvey, for his name hadn't been mentioned around there for some time. He had been briefed about the evil mind-talkers, but neither Mother nor I had thought to mention Harvey to him.

While realizing that Harvey had been quite a problem to me, James said he was not nearly as dangerous as the hairy monsters some people make connection with.

"It wouldn't be so bad," he wrote, "if trespassers could immediately be identified as such, as they would be if you were able to see them, for then all communication could be stopped before they gained too strong a hold. But they're invisible, so who can stick a label on them? Many persons accept as truth what they are told by mischief-makers, thus making a pen pal of a type of spirit in whose company they wouldn't want to be caught dead."

Meanwhile, Mother had apparently gone off on a vacation or something when Anderson was first writing. She evidenced herself later that spring, refreshed enough that she could relieve James Anderson of his duties as correspondent. We polished up her chapter some more and then went over one or two incidents in her childhood. Then one day I said, "Is there anything you particularly want me to add that I haven't said yet?"

"Yes," Mother typed. "I want you to give some more words of warning about the dangers of the Ouija board. We haven't gone into that enough."

"But, Mother, James and I did that while you were gone," I said, somewhat startled. I read her what we had added during the winter.

"It's all right now," she wrote, surprised and pleased.

It seemed to me there was a certain amount of evidence for their existence in what these three communicants did not know about what had been going on with me.

James, when he started writing with me, had never heard of Harvey and how he originally attached himself to me through the Ouija board. Daddy had been aware of very little that had happened to me before he came to visit. Now Mother was surprised at what James and I had written about Ouija while she was away.

If we are going to explain these three different characters with their personal eccentricities and memories as existing within my own subconscious mind, we would once again have to resort to the split-personality theory. But I was once told by a competent psychiatrist friend that whatever I am, I am not schizophrenic.

TWENTY-FOUR

MULTIPLE MISCHANCES

When my invisible writing pool put their final OK on the manuscript as being the best we could do at that time, I started thinking about which publisher in New York to send it to. But my typewriter wrote that I was going to take it to New York myself. Mother said she knew that I would soon move there to live, so there was no use arguing about it.

The idea had no appeal whatever. I'd always fought shy of tackling the biggest city alone, and now it was out of the question because I had very little money left. Reluctantly, however, because she insisted, eventually I began making plans to put the Gingerbread House up for sale, thinking to do my packing during the summer and leave for New York by fall. When my typewriter said instead that I'd be heading north within a month, there seemed no way to comply. Such a big step would take much more preparation than that.

Junior proved Mother right. He hadn't been lively for some time and I'd teased him about getting old, not suspecting that he might be sick. But suddenly his hind legs began to stiffen and he screamed with pain whenever his back was touched, so I rushed him to a vet. He had a slipped disc in his spine and his condition worsened fast. Shots of cortisone relieved his pain only temporarily, and the prognosis was either paralysis or an operation that only possibly *might* be successful.

In Alabama, just off a main highway to New York, was the best veterinary college and hospital in the South, where spinal fusion operations were performed frequently on dachshunds (whose long bodies are especially prone to this disability). So, I packed the car in a rush, left the trailer with an agent to sell, and started north well within the time prophesied.

We caught the head surgeon at the Small Animal Clinic just two days before he was to leave for his summer vacation, and Junior underwent surgery early the next morning. As it was Memorial Day and exactly two years after Nina died, it was doubly difficult for me as I paced the floor of a motel room. The thing I was most afraid of was that Junior was supposed to be taken away from me. It would be complicated to try to work in New York with a dog who hadn't been trained to stay alone. He would probably present many problems there, so I tried to adjust my thinking to the possibility that it might be necessary for me to give him up. But with all my stiff-upper-lipmanship, I couldn't accept the thought of losing my dear little companion of the past seven years, and prayed that he could stay with me.

Junior had a rough time and was even in an oxygen tent for a while, but he was so sure New York was for him that he pulled through in order not to miss the adventure with me. The second day after his operation I made a bed in the front seat of the car, the doctor showed me how to handle the tightly-bandaged little dog, and off we went. We visited my friends Billie and Bob Feagans at their estate outside Lynchburg, Virginia, for ten days while Junior recuperated, then we hit the road again.

Now, besides Junior's sudden damage and subsequent repair, here follows a list of undisastrous misadventures that happened to us within a few brief weeks, and if you didn't know me pretty well by now, you'd be sure I was lying.

The morning we left Lynchburg, a service station attendant looked at the Chevrolet's bulging cargo and put extra air in the back tires to support the load. When the heat of the road and my fifty to sixty mile-per-hour cruising speed made them expand, there were two blowouts of two back tires within two hours. In both instances, when the sharp report sounded and the car became suddenly unmanageable, I was able to hang onto the wheel, pull over to the side of the road, flag down a passerby for assistance, go buy the necessary replacements, and proceed on my way with a minimum of aggravation. But I gave my group of invisible backseat drivers "what-for" nonetheless for letting it happen.

"If you can keep me from wrecking after a blowout, why can't you tell me in the first place not to let the guy put too much air in my tires?" I demanded. Our communication procedures weren't good enough that I could get answers or explanations while in transit. So I had no idea yet that the bad guys were still after me.

I spent the night with Audrey and Joe Soukup in Baltimore and took a shower in their tub, putting all my weight on the built-in soap dish handle to support myself when turning around. The soap dish pulled loose from the wall, and I crashed to the bottom of the tub. Results: one slightly sore muscle and a half-inch cut on my leg. Nothing more.

The next day we skimmed along the Jersey Turnpike and those well-marked throughways that skirt New York on the north and arrived in Stamford, Connecticut, to visit Jean Fonda, who used to work for *Shopping with Susy,* and her husband, Bart. We stayed there a week until I found an apartment in a brand new building in New York City and moved in.

Junior's bandages had been removed, revealing a skinned hide where he'd been shaved from his neck to his tail, and a beautifully healing scar. He handled himself carefully and was convalescing much better than anyone but me had expected, and regained complete use of his back legs. But I still lifted him up and down from things and had been warned never again to allow him to traverse flights of steps under his own steam.

The second morning at Jean's, Junior decided to leave our bedroom before me and start downstairs. I saw him on the top step and shouted, "Wait! You can't do that!" This startled him and he lost his balance, falling down fourteen steps. Frantic, I stood at the top and shrieked, "Oh, God! Help! Save him! Save him!" It was less than two weeks since his operation, and it didn't seem possible that he would survive.

Junior slid and scrambled and skidded on the lightly waxed stairs, never once rolling over on his back. He landed on his feet at the bottom, and looked up at me with a discouraged expression as if to say, "There must be a better way to do it." Then he walked into the kitchen and hit Jean up for some breakfast.

The second week in my new apartment in New York City, in the dark, I fell flat on my face through the open door of the bathroom. Didn't hit the tub, didn't hit the washbasin, didn't even so much as skin my knee.

I fell off a bus a few days later. Missed the top step and picked myself up off the sidewalk, stunned and shaken, but not cracked, chipped or bent, quite able to walk the three weary blocks home. Shortly afterward, I tripped on the metal strip cross the entrance of an old-fashioned elevator and stretched my length on the floor. The only thing I hurt was a finger.

Each time something like this occurred I mentally thanked my invisible associates for their very kind assistance in keeping me from being badly damaged, and also gave them the devil for not assuring that these accidents did not happen in the first place.

"This sort of thing becomes wearing in time," I ranted at them. "I need me all in one piece. I've got to go out and sell a book."

It was not easy to calm down after all the recent stir, but I tried and Mother tried. I sat at my typewriter and what resulted was information I was reluctant to believe—that the bad influences were still with me and that their negative force was strong enough to project those accidents on me.

My guides and spirit helpers weren't just sitting on their hands. They could always go into action immediately to save the day, but it was nonetheless going to be primarily up to me to protect myself. Now that I was more relaxed and able to take charge, I could do what was necessary to get rid of them.

I was going to have to use my thoughts to shelter myself from those earthbound spirits, who viewed me as a threat to them and wanted to get rid of me.

Even with all the experiences with Harvey and Sam and the others, the theory of malicious spirit influence was difficult to take. I just didn't want to get into the habit of ascribing blown tires, slipped discs, horizontal descents from buses, fanny flops in bathtubs, or for that matter, even ingrown toenails or spilt ink, to discarnate delinquents. I knew such beliefs were for people who stick feathers and cow dung in their hair, shake rattles, and wear masks. They could hardly be accepted without indicating atavism. I didn't want my thinking to return to the dark jungles of my origin.

I had been accident-prone for too long, but when doing what my associates told me to do for protection, I became un-accident-prone, and the curtain rang down on my comedy of errors. I settled down in my apartment, took Junior for walks and watched him adjust to big city living with no problems at all, and the days began to pass in the normal, unexciting way that days are supposed to pass.

What my guides told me to do actually sounds so naive that it is difficult for me to describe it here and expect to be taken seriously. Yet at the time I was forced by necessity to accept the simple rules, and I found that they worked so successfully that I have continued to use them since.

I was told to mentally wrap myself in protection at all times. By then I was supposed to be aware of the power of my thoughts, so it should not be too difficult, the guides said, for me to use my mind to keep any intruding entities from getting near enough to harm me. The ways to protect yourself are varied, they told me, but all amount to the same thing.

You mentally enclose yourself in something that acts as a barrier to the intruders. It does not really matter what you cover yourself with, it is the power of your belief in its ability to help you that protects you. It was suggested that I visualize a white light and see myself wrapping it around me as if encircling myself in swaddling clothes. Not one spot must escape my protective efforts. Then, if the belief were strong enough, it would present an impassable wall through which the entities that attempted to harm me could not force an entrance. I must also keep constantly in mind the thought that "Nothing can come near me or in any way influence me that does not come from God in love and peace."

I was later loaned an unpublished manuscript received by automatic writing many years ago—ostensibly from William James—that had wended its way from England to a friend of mine. The material had been received by British medium Maude V. Underhill (1875–1941). Called *The Upward Path,* it is designed to teach people how to live wisely while on Earth so that they will progress more rapidly in spirit planes after death. Many of the statements are of the identical purport and even phrased similarly to those provided by my James. I therefore believe my material comes from the same source, especially since my James accepts the Underhill script as his. He has not acknowledged many of the other published data claiming to come from him that I've asked him about, much of which is unlike what I receive.

The James/Underhill material expands on protection as follows:

> In the early stages of development you become extremely sensitive. It is essential that you should be able to create a psychic sheath through which no undesirable influence can penetrate. Visualize around yourself a transparent, iridescent wall, something like a soap bubble, at arm's length from your body. Think frequently of that sheath until you succeed in feeling it around you

and know that it is strong and elastic in texture. Think of it confidently as a reality, for it can become a very strong one. It is created out of actual invisible matter, which is a substance that may be manipulated by means of thought. Know that all beneficent influences can find access to you through this shell or sheath, but that no evil or disintegrating forces can reach you. Make a habit of working on this protective wall until you feel quite secure from harm. But remember that in order to maintain it intact, you must not entertain the type of thought that would attract evil to you. Fear also weakens your psychic sheath. Doubt about the efficacy of your shield robs it of its power of resistance. However, you may be certain that if you work with a positive mind in creating this shell and maintaining it, you will succeed in rendering yourself immune from outer attacks.

If you ever have any reason to suspect that you are being psychically attacked, keep a light burning by your bedside during the night.

Of course, as one goes on living, one will have occasional misfortunes from time to time. This has nothing to do with such a series of accidents as befell me because of the exertion of the invisible miscreants who were trying to do me in. But whatever the explanation, and whether you believe in all this or not, when I learned to wrap myself in protection, the multiple manifestations of mischance stopped, and they have not resumed.

I have since learned that forming this protective encasing is standard procedure among those who believe in the existence of spirits and have learned how to cope with the malicious ones. It is most frequently described as "enveloping yourself in the white Christ light," although some people think of hardening their auras around them until they become like eggshells that are impenetrable. There are various ways of doing it, but all depend on a firm belief in their success, as the Underhill scripts insist.

Another matter that I came upon without any previous knowledge, only to discover that others everywhere in the world also do it, is spirit missionary work. When I learned to convert Harvey and the other villains, I didn't know it had ever been done by anyone else. Shortly after my arrival in New York, I met a pleasant little woman named Harriett M. Shelton. Shelton, who has since died, was the author of a book called *Abraham Lincoln Returns*. She told me that she sat regularly every day and helped the spirits. Entities that wished to be of service spoke through her when she was in a trance-like state, and what she said was tape recorded. Then she played the tapes frequently so that other misguided spirits who were nearby could hear them.

I told Shelton my experiences with reading Mother's chapter to inform these Earthbound unfortunates. She said that she also happened on this technique of giving assistance without knowing anyone else did such a thing, but that when she went to England she learned that the spiritualist churches there had missionary groups that met regularly for the purpose of passing on exactly this kind of information to unseen entities who needed help. I have since participated in rescue circles in various areas of the country where lost or unenlightened spirits are allowed to possess the medium. Then members of the group attempt to impress them with the fact that they are dead and need to understand where they are and how to adjust to their new situation.

I doubt whether parapsychologists will ever consider such numerous small coincidences as mine as being anything resembling evidence for after-death survival. But to me it was reassuring, at least, to learn that these processes I happened onto are actually used by others who accept belief in spirit survival as a way of life. It was another of the small consolations of which I was to need plenty as my New York existence continued.

TWENTY-FIVE

NEW YORK PSYCHICS
PSYCHE ME OUT

New Yorkers in 1960 did not rush forward to greet me. There were no ticker tape parades; in fact, hardly anybody seemed aware that Ethel Elizabeth Smith had arrived in their midst. The apartment was in a new building on East 76th Street—one large lovely room with a tiny kitchen and bath—and a rent of $143 per month on a two-year lease. I was sure my book would sell quickly so I could keep up the payments. I was determined to approach all problems with positive thinking, so didn't let myself consider any alternatives. After all, a check would be coming in monthly for a while from the woman who bought my trailer.

I felt like a stranger, though. So with my Texas informality I began talking to my neighbors in the elevators and the lobby and in general acting as if the building were a small town. Soon I was dog- and cat-sitting for those who wanted an evening out or a week's vacation. I later learned that this is not quite the way one behaves in New York City, but it produced many friendly contacts at the time.

Publishers to whom my manuscript about my life and early experiences with spirit communication was sent were less than enthusiastic. If there hadn't been a certain amount of encouragement from mediums, I might have folded my tent very quickly and disappeared from the great metropolis.

Locating good sensitives was not easy, however. The scientific organizations in the field, such as the American Society for Psychical Research (A.S.P.R.), which I joined along with its counterpart, the British Society, and the Parapsychology Foundation would not recommend any psychics in the area. It is not the custom for objective groups to take a stand on the ability or integrity of mediums. They're right, because one person may get a good reading and another may be terribly disappointed. One learns that recommendations are seldom wise.

The late Gertrude Tubby was most helpful to me. Tubby, as she was called, was a lively old maid in her eighties who lived in nearby New Jersey. She had been secretary to Dr. James Hyslop of Columbia University when he was the president of the A.S.P.R. many years before, and she was a scientifically oriented believer, as Dr. Hyslop had also been. She knew enough to approach everything psychic from a critical point of view, yet she thought there was so much evidence for survival that it was stupid of researchers not to accept it. Being such a rugged individualist, Tubby was outspoken about it. For years she conducted development classes in her home in Upper Montclair, and I was pleased to be invited. Had it not been such a long bus ride from New York City, I would have attended regularly, instead of only twice.

Members of Tubby's group had progressed well in their mediumship, for she was especially successful as a leader and teacher. Psychic Mary Tallmadge, whom I met there, soon became the leader of a group we formed that met in my New York apartment for years.

In his later work, *The Book of James*, my mentor wrote:

It may not be easy at first to find a meditation group or development class with which to sit. Sometimes the only solution is to start your own among your friends. You will all grow spiritually as you sit together, even though you may not see results of a psychical nature for quite a while. Do not be discouraged. As time goes on, one or more of you may develop more rapidly than the others, and then his or her talents will assist the others to develop, because psychic talent always tends to increase in proportion to the achievements of any one of the group.

When people sit together to meditate and develop, many interested spirits immediately gather to give their assistance. We bring you great measures of love, and we are willing to work endlessly for your advancement. You will all feel this loving warmth to the point that you will come to look forward to your weekly class night with great anticipation.

If you meet for the right purposes and know how to protect yourselves, your safety is assured, so do not worry. In your development circles you are opening up your centers of awareness on several levels. For this reason, during the time that you are making yourselves receptive to spirit influence you must be sure that you are determined to live honestly, earnestly and sincerely. If you maintain self-discipline and keep yourselves on a plane of integrity, purity of motive, and good common sense, with a strong element of humor, your experiences are bound to be pleasant and successful. Earthbound spirits hate happy, well-adjusted people, and they will have nothing to do with you, so your group will be perfectly safe if you follow the techniques I have set down in this book.

When strangers visit a class of this type, members usually attempt to get messages for them. On my first visit to Tubby's, Nancy Craw received automatic writing for me that was heartening. It started off: "There has been great suffering here, but from it has developed a very beautiful, deep, joyous soul. She is exuberant, buoyant, sparkling over with happy enthusiasm. We need so many more like her." This was pleasant enough to gratify me. But there was more yet. "There is love of music and of dancing here—all forms. I get no husband. Much of her family is on the other side. Her father is a lovely person. She is a daughter very much beloved. The initial *M* (Merton, Daddy, of course). "She is a writer, too. She will be a mighty force. Her development at this time is alone. I do not see any understanding companionship here which might help her—no husband. She can write and also lecture . . ."

I returned home from the meeting quite elated. There was just enough factual data in the message to make me hope that the kind words might also be true. At this time I had never given public talks in my life and would have been scared to death to attempt it, but would willingly have made the effort if anyone had asked me. Lecturing later became a big part of my life.

I rode home on the bus from that New Jersey meeting with a most attractive young woman who had also been a guest—Lex Tice, who always captures everyone with her Virginia charm, her enthusiasm, and her pretty pixie face, which is framed by very short, prematurely gray hair. She has remained one of my good friends, and her moral support during my difficult early years in New York was important to me. She even came to see me once during that first autumn when things were particularly drastic and handed me $100, saying, "I felt you might need this to tide you over." That is a rare kind of friend.

The first professional medium I visited was a cultured, gracious former Southern belle, the late Caroline Randolph Chapman. After her initial recounting of the complete history of her life—a tedious habit of hers—I took down in shorthand everything she said to me, and much of it was significant. Although she rambled on and said a few things that were not particularly pertinent, most of what she said was factual and her precognition came true.

I went to Chapman anonymously, a complete stranger who made it a point to say little more than "Yes" and "No," to nod and smile but reveal nothing about myself. Good mediums want you to be cooperative, but if you begin to give them personal information, they invariably say, "Don't tell me. Let me get it." They have a pride of accomplishment that they don't want you to spoil with too many hints. Most people have the wrong idea about mediums, thinking that a visit to one is always a matter of being pumped for information, which is then handed back to you. This is not the practice of the great ones in this field, one of whom Chapman undoubtedly was. It does occur with some mediocre mediums, who ask questions and encourage you to talk, then return to you what you have given them. The only thing Chapman gleaned from my conversation was that I was from the South, and she admitted that my accent had given that away.

After her preliminaries, the first thing she said to me when my message started was, "You will never become unbalanced. If you'd been going to do that, it would have happened before now." I thought about my past year coping with entities who talked in my mind and pushed me around and was somewhat inclined to agree with her. She went on, "You have read a great deal on this subject. You are quite literary and very artistic, have an eagle eye, an analytical and critical mind. You see a lot of flaws in other people. Your spiritual work is helping you to remodel yourself." Yes, Mother had been insisting on that ever since my days in Salt Lake City.

"What you do must be done well or not at all," Chapman went on. "You love a home. You have to have a home of your own even if it is only a 2 x 4." My recently abandoned Gingerbread House was a witness to that. "Dogs and cats like you. You are developing and will be a medium. Remember my words; you will uplift the fallen. You will enlighten them and give them help."

This was all very fine, but enough of the small talk, I thought. Let's get down to something evidential. She did, saying, "There is a grandmother here on your mother's side. You never saw her." This was correct. She then gave me three specific names—Anna, Jane and Charles—who were all Mother's relatives. She added, "There is something about your name that is a little different. There has been a change in your name." (Ethel to Susy.)

"Have you been married once?" she asked. "I see a broken ring over your head. You had a wonderful mother. You were always very close to her, more like a sister. She had an abundance of beautiful hair at one time." My greatest disappointment in Mother had been when she cut that gorgeous long auburn mane and began to wear it short.

"Are you doing any writing at all?" the medium asked. I was not, at the moment, so I hesitated. She pushed on with it. "Are you a writer? Do you do literary work? There is something you are writing or have written that is going to be published. It is only the beginning of your writing. Mother has helped you a bit on your book."

After a few comments about my wonderful guides, but no names for them, Chapman shook her head in amazement. "I don't know anybody who has had such a reading as this . . . you are getting so much help in your life from spirits, and they are all here. You seem to be standing very much alone at the present moment, but you know you are not alone."

Chapman said that someone named Helen was going to be of great service to me. She was right in that, too, because it was Mother's friend from her Front Royal, Virginia, days, Helen Simpson Phillips who, you might say, launched my career. She was a head nurse at Mt. Sinai Hospital when I first arrived in New York, and she helped me find my apartment and acquire some inexpensive furniture. While so doing she told me so many of her own interesting psychic experiences—some of which were verified by other people involved—that I wrote an article about her. When it came out the next summer in *Tomorrow* magazine, it was my first published piece about the psychic field.

Among several other names Chapman gave me were William and Robert—my great-grandfather. These are common names; one cannot get too excited about receiving them. When they crop up as frequently as they do for me, however, there may be a reason.

"You are going to teach and preach immortality," she added. "You will relieve the fear of death for many. You are

172

going to prevent several suicides. You are destined to help people. You have a world of work to do in writing and investigating. Lots of research."

When Chapman asked for a question, I suggested she try to give me my mother's name. "I'll work on that," she said. Then after a pause, "It wasn't Elizabeth?" That was a direct hit, but I had hoped she would give me the name I liked better. I said, "Not quite." Then she said, "Betty. Didn't she die of cancer?" Again I replied, "Not quite," for Mother had cancer at the time she died and the doctor told me it would soon have caused her death if her heart hadn't given out first. Chapman added, "Her heart was bad, too." Then, she gave another prediction: "You will soon meet a professional man, a lawyer, who will be of help to you and play a big role in your life."

The medium finished my interview with a surprise that capped the whole thing. "James Anderson," she said. "He has given you some very definite things."

In a critical review of this one might say, "It was only telepathy involved here. Your own mind was the source of all the information." Telepathy is a genuine supernormal feat and nothing to be sneezed at. Much of what mediums get must involve it. Yet her prediction about my writing, with special reference to all the research and the teaching of immortality, was only later realized, on a long-range basis. Her statement that I would meet a lawyer who would be important to me came true almost immediately.

Shortly after my visit to Chapman I made a week's trip to Onset, Massachusetts, with Tubby and Shelton (the one who talks to Lincoln) to attend an Arthur Ford seminar. I was eager for a reading from him, for even in 1957 this medium had a high reputation. I had told no one in New York any data about my family, hugging personal information to my bosom because it might bring evidence from psychics. After our arrival at Onset, I attempted to arrange for a private sitting with Ford before he had any chance to learn anything about me from my two garrulous companions, who were his close friends and might unwittingly reveal to him some of the few little things they had learned about me on our trip. I was to wonder about this later.

Almost the first thing Arthur said to me was, "Who's Ethel?" Then he went on with the following: "There is a lady who says you were named after her but you changed your name. You were named after your grandmother." Yes, Elizabeth. "She must have been Scotch. Annie and Jeannie, an aunt of yours." I greeted Aunt Anna. "She was very fond of you. She tells me that your life has been broken up into difficult emotional situations. You made an unfortunate marriage and got a divorce. 'On the Earth plane,' she says, 'I was against divorce,' but you had to have it to keep your self-respect. For a while you built a cynical wall around you."

Then Arthur said, "You were born with a great artistic ability. From the time you were a young girl you have liked to go off with paper and pencil and in later years a typewriter. You think better with a typewriter." I always maintain that, but how did Arthur Ford know it?

He went on, "So far what you have been doing has been preparation, training, and in the next year or so immediately ahead of you, you are going to write some remarkable things. You are really a good writer.

"Do you know who Betty is? Was she Betty Smith? She says her fingers are straight now." (Mother had arthritis in her finger joints that had been very painful.)

Ford then focused on my current problem: "Right now you need to do very much about your financial situation. You have worked as a secretary. You are going to get another job, soon. You do have some remarkable psychic powers. They are slow developing. When the psychic flow begins to come through you, you begin to question and you defeat the flow. Don't try to analyze it as it comes. You have this objective way of dealing with things. Your big problem now is to settle down to serious writing and get yourself a job that will ease up on the financial situation."

Shelton had been arguing with me about this on the way up on the train. While I had told her nothing about my past or my family, I *had* mentioned living on an inheritance that had dwindled to only a few hundred dollars. I was also mentioned that I had done secretarial work but hated it and didn't intend to subject myself to it again, because I was determined to make my living as a writer.

A wealthy woman, Harriet Shelton was horrified that I should be so unrealistic. She began insisting that I get a job immediately. When Ford told me the same thing in almost the same way, I was certain that she had coached him to say it to me when she had made my appointment. I lost faith in him completely at that moment. Although enjoying his teachings at the seminar, I was reserved with him after that whenever we chanced to meet. I felt that my sitting with him had been a farce.

Reading my notes later I saw that he made many hits on matters he had no normal way of knowing, short of doing a great deal of research about me—which he could not have done because he had not even known I was coming, much less who I was. And for that matter, who was I? Why should it have been worth his while to try to investigate the background of this stranger even if he'd had the opportunity? Possibly he got the data by telepathy, but it is more likely that it came as it purported to come—from the entities in question. Ford was a medium of genuine talent who did not have to resort to devious methods to get information about his sitters. I am sure now that the personal information he gave me came psychically. I observed a great deal in his life and experiences after I came to know him better that has altered entirely my first negative response to him.

Arthur Ford was no more impressed than I at our first encounter. Several years later after a Spiritual Frontiers Fellowship meeting in New York, I went up to him and identified myself. My first paperback, *ESP*, had just come out and he said shortly, "Oh, yes, Susy Smith. I've just read your book *ESP*. You're a lot brighter than I thought you were."

Arthur and I later became good friends, and had long and fascinating chats whenever we got together. I didn't hold that earlier remark against him, willing as I am to accept the occasional crack if it is constructive.

TWENTY-SIX

I SEE JUNIOR AGAIN

I was beginning to enjoy my New York contacts, and learning to be familiar with the big city was enchanting, if exhausting. My car had been sold after three days, because keeping it in the garage was expensive and leaving it on the street required an unending struggle to find parking places. But waiting for buses and subways, and then usually having to stand in them when they came along, was no help to muscles and joints already made uncomfortable by the climate.

Junior settled into city routines, however, as if he had been born to them. He looked forward to his daily walks, when he could investigate the new and fascinating smells and commune with neighboring dogs also hiking along on their leashes. He remained inside peacefully the rest of the time. He was middle-aged by then and not needing to be too active. A Hungarian doctor friend who lived in the next apartment kept an ear out for me. He reported that when I was gone from home for long periods during the day, at about eleven A.M., he could hear Junior howling "Oooo" a few times. That's the only unfavorable comment my pet ever made about New York living.

My big problem was financial. My reluctance to apply for a job wasn't just a stupid refusal to give up and go to work. It was also the understanding that I would never be able to tackle rush hour traffic if I took a secretarial job, and a hesitancy to try to compete with experienced, established local newspaper personnel if I attempted to get interesting work.

Upon selling the trailer for $1,200, I had accepted a deposit and payments, and was trying to live on the $200-per-month checks. In September the final payment arrived—and the check bounced. There was at that time $8.50 in my bank account, and the rent was due.

Having found that writing with Mother on the typewriter was close to impossible in New York—she said that vibrations there are not conducive to communication—I had been almost out of touch with her. I didn't dare try to open my mind to hear from her mentally. Those intruders might still be lurking, and I wasn't about to give them the opportunity to penetrate my surrounding white light of protection. Now, however, in desperation, I sat at my typewriter and said, "Mother, what'll I do?"

Except to identify herself to my satisfaction, she didn't say much. But what she said was to the point: "Have you thought of your shell jewelry?"

I thought about my shell jewelry for quite a while, getting out my remaining pieces and looking at them. They were shells that had been dyed green and red and made into pretty little Christmas trees and bells and wreath pins and earrings decorated with rhinestones, pearls and sequins. They were high fashion enough to sell to classy New Yorkers, so I took them down to Saks Fifth Avenue, Lord and Taylor, and Macy's Little Shop boutique and got orders for $500. I rushed a request for supplies off to Florida and when they came, sat day and night gluing this decorative jewelry. And I fell in love with Jack Paar, whose *Tonight Show* enlivened my evenings. I finally got up nerve enough to apply to his program, which was at that time featuring people with interesting occupations. My shells attracted enough attention that I was on his show twice, and I managed to get a few words in about my psychic interests as well. These were the first of many later TV appearances, which publishers got for me to publicize my books.

About that time I also got a job as secretary in the pathology department at Lenox Hill Hospital, which was only a couple of blocks from my apartment. After my Christmas shell-making orgy was over, I applied for a grant from the Parapsychology Foundation, run by the famous medium Eileen Garrett. I had read F. H. W. Myers's remarkable two-volume text, *Human Personality and Its Survival of Bodily Death*, and thought it could only be improved by tightening it up and eliminating half of the material in it. Garrett agreed that it should be done and gave me a grant to accomplish it. After completing that at nights while I worked at the hospital during the day, I received grants from her to do two other books. I was off and running on my big authorship career. Of great help to me was Martin Ebon, then executive secretary of the Foundation and now a well known author/editor of about eighty books. He is the one who published my first psychic piece—about Helen Simpson Phillips—in *Tomorrow* magazine. I give him credit for many of the other good things that have happened to me. He put agent Donald MacCampbell in touch with me, and Donald sold many of my books to big publishers like Putnam, Prentice-Hall and Macmillan.

I spent seven years in wonderful New York, having an interesting time sitting in development classes to improve my psychic abilities, going to the opera and concerts and shows (the best thing about the Big Apple, for my money), taking an art class at the New School for Social Research and getting my first books published. And I might as well admit it: I had a gall bladder operation and then two kidney stones removed, but who's counting?

Then the light of my life went out. My dear little Junior died. Bill Hanemann wrote after hearing the news, "He was such a manly little fellow." After that I didn't enjoy New York much, and I took the opportunity to go to Europe. A friend who had traveled a great deal as an Army colonel but must have been somehow misled as to realities told me you could travel in Europe on ten dollars a day. What a farce! Anyway, I broke my right foot in Italy and spent a large part of the summer in hospitals and then hobbling around with neither side functioning very well. I'm skipping the foreign details because nothing noticeably psychic went on in my life until I arrived in England.

I tottered into London in early September, exhausted from trying to struggle across Europe with no feet and no funds. That's not the way to travel.

The next morning, I woke up early in my hotel room, then seemed to drift into a light doze. Suddenly I was with Junior. My dog saw me, perked up his ears, then leaped on me with his usual affectionate enthusiasm. Holding him in my arms as he joyously licked my face and expressed his happiness at seeing me, I just as delightedly hugged and petted his squirming body. I asked myself what the hell was going on.

"This is not a dream," I declared emphatically, and it wasn't. It was in no way dreamlike. Was it an out-of-body experience? It must have been. I had written much about astral projection and had come during my research to have no doubt of its authenticity. The aspect of astral projection that involves seeing a deceased friend, pet or relative occurs often enough to give it credence, and sometimes evidence is brought back of its veracity. Similar travels were the basis of Swedenborg's vast amount of information. Now it had happened to me.

I'd been told that Junior continued to stay with me after his death because well loved pets sometimes remain with their owners. Mother said she was taking good care of him for me. I had not doubted that someday the dog would be with me again, but a visit so soon was unexpected. Yet there he was, and there I was, and it was not a dream.

"I'm really here with Junior and we both know it," I thought. "I am awake and aware. There is no doubt about that either." I was sure that what had occurred was so exciting it would last me a lifetime. It has. I can still feel that little dog in my arms, and I have a better understanding of a whole new aspect of psychical phenomena.

Another rewarding English experience was my visit to the retired medium Gladys Osborne Leonard at her home in Kent. Because I was at the time writing the book *The Mediumship of Mrs. Leonard*, I was invited to spend the weekend as her guest, and she was a delight in every way. Gladys Leonard was one of the two or three greatest mediums in history. She had been studied for over fifty years by the Society for Psychical Research, and every word that came through her when she was in trance was recorded and analyzed for the vast amount of authentic survival evidence it provided. In her late seventies at the time we met, this great lady looked and acted like a woman in her fifties. Her serenity was beautiful to observe, and we had an immediate rapport. I left her hoping that some of her tranquility and composure had rubbed off on me, but not suspecting that any of her talent had. Yet that very day my most mediumistic experience occurred.

Before I left New York, Renée Dubonnet had given me the name of a British woman; I was to find out why she didn't write to Renée. She'd told me nothing about her friend, and I had been in England for some days and had not yet bothered to call her. After returning to my London hotel from Kent, an immediate urge possessed me to phone Renée's friend. When her maid said she was out, I left my number.

That evening at five the woman returned my call, saying she would love to meet me but she was leaving the next day for a vacation in Italy. Not caring about seeing her, I nonetheless found myself insisting, "Oh, I won't take but a few minutes of your time."

"I have no way to entertain you," she demurred. "I don't even have any liquor in the house to offer you a drink." Nothing of the sort was in the least necessary, I replied, adding that it would be possible for me to come right over.

When I walked out of the telephone booth in the lobby of this rural, home-style hotel, the manager was standing near the front door. I asked him how to find the address, somewhere across London, and he said, "I'm leaving now in my car and will be driving right by the house. I'll be glad to take you with me."

One thing you eventually learn is that there's no use fighting it. When a bunch of those etheric entities get onto something specific, you might as well relax and go along gracefully.

Magician Aleister Crowley said in his *Confessions*: "It is impossible to perform the simplest act when the gods say 'no'." When one learns not to push ahead when it is obvious the "gods" are against it, one can live much more successfully. This is also true in reverse. When the gods, or spirits, or guardian angels, or whatever it is that takes hold of your life at times, say "yes," your path is smooth before you.

When I arrived at Renée's friend's house, she began pouring forth her woes to me. This nice person, probably in her early forties, had recently had so many unhappy events in so short a period of time that they almost overwhelmed her, and she was at a point of desperation where they erupted to anyone who would listen. As a captive audience, I learned that she had lost her husband to another woman, and he had taken her family furniture and valuable possessions with him when they got the divorce—as he legally could do in England. Then her sister died of cancer, and to top it all off, one of her beloved twin Siamese cats fell out of a window and was killed, and the other died of grief. This woman had troubles.

As I listened attentively, my head became very light and dizziness almost overwhelmed me. Since she hadn't been able to provide me with any stronger refreshments than a tiny glass of sherry, I didn't know what was the matter, until a firm impression came that her sister wanted to talk to her. Would my hostess be receptive to such a notion? Could I just say to this stranger, "By the way, your dead sister wants to speak to you?" She might take me gently but forcibly by my ear and show me to the door.

I went at it gingerly, saying first, "I don't know if you are at all interested in ESP and psychical research, but I write books about that field." She replied that she was very interested, and that helped. Then I tentatively offered that sometimes I was a bit mediumistic myself. That didn't seem to shock her; becoming bolder I said, "In fact, your sister would like to try to talk to you now. Do you mind?"

Grateful when she said she didn't, I laid my head against the back of my chair and let the light-headedness take over. I remained conscious, my actual thinking apparatus very alert as it sat there inside my brain listening to the words that began to flow through my mouth. Monitoring everything that was said, I was horrified when statements were made that might or might not have been true. After all, I could have been making a terrible clown of myself, yet my mouth would not stop.

What was said at first went along with my thinking and could easily have been coming from me, for the lady was told to stop reliving her grief and talking so much about it. But then came the words, "When you are in Italy, try not to tell anyone about your problems. Be sure to take your oil paints and spend as much time as possible painting. That will be wonderful therapy for you."

Listening to this, I thought, "You don't know whether or not she paints." Certainly the walls revealed no amateur art, and she hadn't mentioned it.

As several other statements of a like nature were made, I became more and more apprehensive, but I was unable to take control of my mouth to apologize.

The finish actually startled me. The sister said, "Mother and I are with you all the time and love you very much and do all we can to help you. Trust us and make yourself receptive to us." Her mother might live right around the corner! "You don't know if she's even dead," wailed my mind. "This girl will think you're an idiot!"

Then everything cleared up suddenly. Not dizzy any more, I opened my eyes warily, prepared to be greeted by any kind of dirty look. Instead, Renée's friend was radiant. She hardly seemed to be the same person.

"You don't know what you've done for me," she exulted. "This is the nicest thing that's ever happened to me."

"But was it correct?" I asked. "Was what I said true? Are you an artist? Is your mother dead? Were there really any hits?"

"Everything you said was true, and the advice was so wise that I promise to adopt it," she declared. As I left, she reiterated her happiness at the messages. It was evident that mediumship does have rewards, which might be commensurate with the effort it takes to become receptive.

TWENTY-SEVEN

THE POEM I NEVER WROTE

During my last three weeks in London I had sittings with two well known mediums. The first was Douglas Johnson, who was one of the day's most respected sensitives because of his willingness to work with parapsychologists in their efforts to learn more about a psychic's abilities and talents. He and I later became friends during his various trips to America. At the time of my first visit we were complete strangers, and I went in anonymously. Yet Douglas Johnson told me thirty-five things that could be verified, beginning with a good description of Mother and a close approximation of her name—the first initial *E* and then later "Binny or Bitty."

He said, "She's showing me a manuscript. Have you anything to do with writing?" He told me there would be a lot of platform work in my future. Then he said, "It hasn't been a very lucky trip for you. Something to do with Italy." How true!

Douglas predicted that there would be an adjustment in my personal and material life when I returned to America—a physical movement of home and surroundings. "You may not be contemplating this at this time," he said, and I certainly was not, for there was a three-year lease on my Greenwich Village apartment. Shortly after my return, however, Emmy Pontzen and I decided to share a larger place, my apartment was sublet, and we moved in together on East 36th Street.

The other medium I visited anonymously in London was Elizabeth Bedford, and one of the first things she told me was that I mustn't give up my home, not yet. She proved to be right, for sharing with Emmy turned out to be an uncomfortable situation for both of us. Her German firmness and my Southern casualness were constantly at odds.

There was one amusing psychic incident that came out of our effort to share an apartment. One Sunday afternoon we had a slight fracas. Determined not to let it grow into a full-fledged fight, I took a Valium, went into my room, closed the door and lay down on the bed.

Almost immediately words started flooding into my mind that were so surprising they compelled me to pay attention to them. I had never once in my life dwelt on the subject of the discourse that now presented itself, yet what was said would have to be the result of some kind of genuine cogitation from someone.

I soon realized that what was coming was a poem, something for which I personally have no writing aptitude. In fact, since the age of ten, I haven't written anything more poetical than an occasional dirty limerick. Yet here was an original free-verse poem flooding into my mind.

After a few moments, I scurried over to my typewriter to let the muse record her effort, which produced the following result:

Oh, great gray-bearded ones
With your visions of God and his glories
Help us to know you better.
For the needs of modern science
And research of the phenomena called psychic
Will you clarify for us the conditions surrounding you
At the moment of your startling revelations?

Do not corrupt the purity of your concept with naive
        credence,

But project forthwith as upon a motion picture screen
The specific details of your supernormal happenings,
Making each succinct and to the point,
Unclouded by wishful thinking or childhood traumas.
Convince us, ancients, that imagination played no
      major role
In your accounts.
Rally for your defense observers of your grand
      experiences,
And if such be not forthcoming
Then submit affirmations from character witnesses
Who have known you from your youth
And found in you no bad or distrustful thing.
Think carefully, please, each one of you
And each one tell us true
If all events, on solemn reconsideration,
Were as awe-inspiring as initially affirmed by you.
Or do you now wish to change, perchance,
      your testimony?
Analyze your mental moods at the time of
      your visions

Were you, perhaps, overwrought from contemplating
The beauties of your world, or the grandeur of God?
Had lack of sleep, or fasting, left you
In an exhausted and fanciful state?
Or, conversely, did an overindulgence in sweetmeats
Cause you restless dreams?
Is it possible that knowledge of the gentle body of a
      Hebrew maiden
Had left you sated, and susceptible?
Could native wine cooled in an earthen jar
Have gone to your head before your abdomen?
Or were you drunk only with love of your God?

Assemble, you great prophetic scribes and orators
And with ringing rhetoric and resounding rodomontade
Apprise us of what took place in fact.

Was that wheel, Ezekiel, truly way up in the middle
     of the air?
Or had some curiously sublime cloud formation
     exalted you
And corrupted your senses?
And, Jacob, your ladder—
In the light of sober afterthought
Did it really extend all the way to Heaven?
Give us, Jonah, once again
The dimensions of your sacred whale,
Uncolored by fantasy
And uncluttered with desire to startle or
     impress your listeners.

You must know, gentlemen, that in this present day
Of science, psychology, and supreme conformity
Your unsupported testimony cannot be accepted
Without full corroborating details.

TWENTY-EIGHT

LARRY KING, REGIS AND A POLTERGEIST

Emmy and I subleased our apartment and went our separate ways shortly after that poem made its appearance. I flew to Calgary and went on to Banff and Lake Louise, of whose special beauty I had always heard. Then I took the train to Vancouver and Seattle, where there were some ghosts to be apprehended for a new book, and to investigate the medium Keith Milton Rhinehart. Lots of interesting experiences occurred there, including another psychic's confirming the name of the pen pal who had called himself James Anderson originally. One day after he had typewritten an entire page without signing it, he said at the bottom: "Take this to your medium and ask for his psychic impression of who wrote it." I did this, and Keith held the paper to his forehead for a moment and then cried out, "William James? Is he one of your guides?"

I enjoyed working with the people in Seattle and became convinced that Keith at least part of the time exhibited genuine mediumistic talent. Yet sometimes he came up with such scuzzy stuff it could hardly be credible. Still, he paid for a trip to Hawaii for me to speak to his groups there, which I greatly appreciated. After that I spent the winter in Los Angeles. By spring I had bought a small car and was on my way around the rest of the country, doing more research for my book *Prominent American Ghosts*. June found me in Saco, Maine, wondering where to go to write it now that I had all the material at hand.

Fortunately, I met author, astrologer and yoga teacher Marcia Moore. Being familiar with my work, Marcia gave me an unusually warm welcome. During our conversation I mentioned my impasse.

"I'm ready to settle down now and write *Prominent American Ghosts*, but where?" I asked. Marcia responded with a brilliant idea.

"Come home with me," she said. "My husband and I live in a big house on the coast near York Beach. We could let you have a suite of rooms for as long as you like."

Marcia was so charming, her husband Mark Douglas so nice, her home so inviting and her invitation so sincere that I accepted, rooming and boarding there for nearly three months. The house was one of those huge twenty-room "summer cottages" so often built on the seashore in the early part of this century. The empty servants' wing alone was larger than most modern dwellings. Marcia and Mark lived and wrote their books in this enormous abode, rattling around like seeds in a maraca when her children were away at summer camp or boarding school.

I settled down with delight at such a favorable spot in which to work, spending most of each day at my typewriter before a window overlooking that famous rock-bound coast.

As I sat at my desk watching rolling waves, all was well . . . in daylight. As the tides went out at dusk, my back, exposed to the large bedroom and the larger hallway beyond my open door, began to chill. I didn't want to be rude and close myself in, but the huge dark hall opened into a stairwell that was at least fifty feet across and extended from the front foyer up to the gaping third floor and yawning attic—an expanse that could have been inhabited by any number of ghastly ghouls at night. No matter how much I worked to control my mind, flurries along my spine were inevitable as I sat alone writing ghost stories.

My only companions in the house—Mark and Marcia—spent most of their time working in their bedroom-and-office suite at the far end of the hall, a good block away. Mark, an editor who was helpfully reading my manuscript as it was produced, had a habit of walking softly up the hall and then abruptly saying "Susy!" just outside my door. My tendency to leap out of my skin had considerable practice until I trained Mark to jingle the sconce in the hall by my door or hum a little tune to announce his coming.

Daytimes the massive mansion, charming in sunlight, was enjoyable. The ocean was too cold for swimming, but I sunned on the rocks every warm day, and attempted to learn some yoga for exercise. I almost got my fill of Maine lobster, caught in little pots bouncing on the billows outside my window. I made pastel sketches of the Nubble lighthouse on York Point way across the bay. My book was written under what might be considered ideal conditions. Except at night.

In September came time for another big decision. My work was finished and sent to the publisher; now where to go from Maine? With no family to return to and no established home because of all my traveling, I always had to ask, "Where do I go now?" It was frequently necessary to have special help about this. Even though I tried to live my life as if God had me in His pocket, sometimes when a big decision must be made, more prayerful effort had to be expended in order to get specific results.

The answer came so promptly as to be miraculous, for in just a few days I received a letter from Margaret Sanders, who was planning a trip around the world for about six months and wondered if her friend Susy would like to live in and take care of her Miami apartment while she was away. My response was immediate; Margaret joined me in Maine, I sold my car, and we drove to Miami in her Mercedes Benz, which was at my disposal until her return from her round trip.

Yes, my friend had done well since our days in Salt Lake City. So had her "finger-lickin' good" father, Colonel Sanders.

So the elegant penthouse apartment I moved into in Miami was filled with expensive antiques, as well as Margaret's sculptured heads. My time there was spent working on two new books. After her return, I took an apartment of my own and remained in Southern Florida for over three years.

Brief mention should be made of a few interesting psychic experiences that occurred during this time. Shortly after my arrival in Miami, I attended a meeting at which medium Eunice VanWyk gave a talk. Afterward she had a message for me from someone named Gertrude.

"She died this summer," Eunice said. To save my life, I couldn't at the moment think of any Gertrude who had died. "She died while you were in New England." Eunice said, and how did she know I'd been there? Then she gave a date in July. When I disclaimed any knowledge of this Gertrude, Eunice insisted, "Yes, you do know her. Gertrude Tub . . . "

"Of course!" I interrupted her with an exclamation. "Miss Tubby. How nice of her to come!"

I had read in the *Spiritual Frontiers Fellowship* magazine that Tubby had died in July. Eunice may have read that magazine, but how could she have known that Tubby and I had been acquainted long ago in New York?

Two other mediums, Harry Levy and his wife Marjorie, were said to have physical phenomena at their home, so a group of us met there a few times with high hopes of seeing trumpets fly in the air, or anything else sensational. We didn't have that kind of luck, but once a table levitated while we were sitting around with our hands on it. As it was quite dark, it was not easy to be sure just how the table lifted—whether alone or with some judicious prodding from underneath—but it did rise up into the air to the height of our shoulders and there was no evidence that I could see or feel of any kind of trickery.

My surprise was not at this, but later, at a response that came when the table began to tip in answer to our questions.

Before the tipping started, Marjorie said she saw a woman bringing me a rose. This may perhaps have been that same flowery female that the psychic in Los Angeles in 1955 had mentioned. I was still sure it wasn't Mother, so I asked Marjorie to describe her. When she mentioned the long brown hair, parted in the middle and pulled back smoothly over the ears into a bun on the neck, and the beautifully serene face, I recognized my Aunt Ivy.

After this, while we sat with our hands on the table and repeated the letters of the alphabet, the table rose up and stood on one leg with the other three up in the air. It would come down flat on the floor with a rap when we reached the letter it wanted. In this way several names were spelled out and messages were given for various persons.

When it came my turn I asked, "With whom have I had communication at home?" In my mind was the James Anderson/William James controversy. Perhaps the table might spell out William's name and thus give me one more in the series of confirmations of his identity.

My first response was satisfactory. The table spelled "Mother."

"Who else?" I asked increasingly eager to get the desired verification.

"Harvey."

It had been ten years since Harvey was last with us, and he was seldom recalled. No one in that group had heard of my experience with him, and the Levys knew nothing personal about me. Was Aunt Ivy sending me a message in this unusual manner? Was anybody? If not, where did it come from?

When I lived in Coral Gables, an acquaintance dropped in occasionally who had no interest whatever in ESP or related areas. He stated firmly, "My rabbi says there's no life after death." That was enough for him.

Once when this man happened by, I got out the Ouija board to entertain him, and he endured it out of curiosity as to how it worked. He soon had it all figured out. "You push it," he asserted.

My "No, I don't" was to no avail, so I invented a new technique of Ouija board operation—placing my hand lightly on top of his hand, which was on the planchette. The little pointer began to race across the board and indicate letters, but as I had purposely sat at the back of the board so that he could see what was going on, I did not observe what was spelled. In fact, I just presumed it was producing nonsense as it usually does when getting warmed up. After it stopped writing, the man took his hand off the planchette and sat stupidly staring at me. Finally he said, "Do you know what happened?"

"No," I replied, "Did it spell anything that made sense?"

"It only wrote the name of a dead uncle of mine and gave me greetings from him," he said. He didn't want to work the board anymore after that. He seemed disconcerted. Before he left, however, he had arrived at an explanation that satisfied him. "You pushed it," he said.

Among all my other seminal activities of this period, I appeared on Larry King's radio show twice while he was just starting out in Miami; and on a trip to San Diego I was interviewed by Regis Philbin, whose program then originated from a nightclub. Both men were pleasant, but who knew they would ever become such prominent television personalities?

My poltergeist came to me through a radio program, and it turned out to be a most curious and entertaining event. Parapsychologists maintain that the occasional instances of a house being taken over by flying objects are caused by psychokinesis, an unusual force that occurs in the mind of a person who has an intense amount of repressed emotion. Spiritualists tend to believe that what is flinging bric-a-brac about is more likely a prankish spirit using and directing this flow of energy. I hardly suspected or even hoped for an opportunity to see such things for myself. But on the afternoon of January 12, 1967, while I was being interviewed by Bill Smith on WKAT's *Talk of Miami* program, a young woman called saying that beer mugs and boxes were flying from the shelves of the warehouse where she worked. What did I recommend they do to stop this annoyance? *Stop it?* If a poltergeist had gone berserk there, I wanted to see it in action!

"Just keep cool and hang on until I can get there," I told her. And they did. Or rather, it hung on to them. It remained with them for twenty-three days altogether. During this time I happened to be right in the midst of much of the action, starting the next morning–Friday the thirteenth–an ideal date on which to begin such a singular enterprise. I began in the office interviewing each of the employees, and they all spouted the same refrain as the manager, Al Laubheim: "I don't believe it, but something we can't see is making a shambles of this warehouse." Just then there was a thud, and everyone, with me trailing, rushed to the large back room where ten-cent-store souvenirs were stacked on rows of shelves. There we found two young men and a girl pointing excitedly to a box lying on its side in an aisle. From it were spilling a number of plastic pencil sharpeners.

"It just fell all by itself," the frightened girl cried. The boys nodded alarmed agreement.

The first thing I personally observed occurred a short while later when I was in the warehouse with Al and the two stock room boys, who were busily stacking boxes on the shelves. They were close to me and directly in the line of my vision when we heard something fall across the room. It proved to be a box of rubber daggers. While the four of us— the only persons there—were gathered around the daggers, examining the shelf from which they had fallen, there was a crash in the first aisle, some twenty-five feet away. There we found a china sailfish ashtray smashed to bits on the cement floor.

Things like this, which went on every few hours during the day, revolved around handsome Puerto Rican refugee Julio, one of the stockroom boys. Although he was never close when they flitted about, they didn't occur when he was out of the room, either. At first he was as frightened as everyone else—I felt his pounding heart a few times. Later I think he began to get cocky about all the attention, for by then police were in and about frequently, the media were always around, and crowds were pushing so hard at the big plate glass front windows that Al was afraid they'd shatter. Our picture, with Al showing a goofily amazed Susy a shattered glass at our feet, was on the front page of the *Miami Herald*.

I phoned my friend Bill Roll, then project director of the Psychical Research Foundation in Durham, and he arrived the next day. After that, one or more of the various parapsychologists he brought were usually there from time to time observing. If you like crowds and attention, get a poltergeist.

One day when Julio and I were alone at the front desk during lunch hour, I placed a glass beer mug on a high shelf far across the room. I hadn't gotten back to the boy before it crashed, and it didn't break. Another time, when a lot of people were in the room busy at one thing or another, I walked down an aisle and my skirt somehow reached out and pulled a big box of nails off their perch. I could go on and on, but this isn't the place. I'll conclude the Miami poltergeist with one account that brought excellent evidence.

Patrolman David J. Sackett and magician Howard Brooks had one of the best-observed incidents to report. Brooks, a professional magician for some thirty-five years, had been a friend of Al's for even longer, but their relationship nearly broke up over the poltergeist. When Al began to talk about the crazy happenings at his business, Howard taunted him unmercifully.

"What kind of gullible fool are you?" he asked. "You obviously have an employee who's playing tricks on you. I can make things crash from shelves, too, when nobody is near them. Just a little piece of string and some spirit gum will do it easily. Or some dry ice. Any magician can do this."

While Howard Brooks was still in his truculent mood, one day he and Officer Sackett experienced something that convinced them both of the genuine supernormality of the occurrences. Sackett had brought in his wife on his day off to see the curious things he'd been telling her about. They happened to be standing at the south end of aisle four. Howard Brooks was at the north end of the warehouse, looking toward them. At that moment, two boxes fell from the top shelf into aisle four. Although nobody saw them actually leave the shelf, both Sackett and his wife and Brooks observed them in flight and watched them land on the floor, one neatly on top of the other.

When Brooks and Sackett rushed to the shelf, there was no evidence of foreign substances of any kind that could have caused the boxes to move. No string, no spirit gum, no dry ice—nothing small enough to go unnoticed—could have moved objects so large. The two boxes, which, as Sackett noted, "remained curiously together as they fell," weighed four pounds.

"Paraphernalia," Brooks said, "which would move that weight would have to have been visible when we arrived there immediately afterward." Brooks admitted that he was sold on the supernatural explanation for the phenomenon. Officer Sackett told me later that he knows that nobody was near enough to that shelf to move those boxes, and he knows that boxes don't propel themselves from shelves alone . . . but he also knows what he saw.

How our invisible playmate, the poltergeist, must have been laughing at us as we worried and wondered and tried to explain! He continued to produce his phenomena almost under our noses, or at least as soon as our backs were turned.

Al wasn't amused at the damage. After he fired Julio on the twenty-third day, the unseemly activity stopped, but it followed the youth to jobs in two other Miami stores, where the managers told me of their amazement at what they saw. Later I convinced Julio to go to Durham, for observation. One evening when technicians from Dr. Rhine's Duke laboratory were in a room with the boy, a vase fell off a table in the hall outside while no one else was in the building. Shortly after his return, Julio married his pretty Cuban girlfriend and they took off for Puerto Rico. He has never been heard from since, to my knowledge.

It is no wonder this has gone down in the records as a case of special value, because it was possible to put the involved protagonist under controlled conditions and still observe the supernormal activity going on around him.

TWENTY-NINE

JAMES WRITES A BOOK OF HIS OWN

By February 1967 books of mine were ready to come out under the auspices of several good publishers. I was living in a small, easy-to-care-for apartment in Miami's salubrious climate, with a swimming pool outside my front door for exercise and relaxation, and I was not unduly pressured either for time or money. I was sitting regularly once a week with a psychic development circle, but was not aware that my psychic abilities had improved to any great extent. In fact, I had no idea what my current capabilities were, having been unable to try communication for a long while due to the excitement of chasing ghosts and poltergeists.

On Wednesday, February 22, I had dinner at the home of my friend Anne Fansler, a highly educated woman who was a librarian at the University of Miami. During the evening we decided to meditate together for a while. When we were sitting quietly and making ourselves receptive, we both began to have an unusually elated feeling as if something wonderful were about to happen. I almost burst from my skin with the joy that took hold of me.

Then a voice began to speak through my lips, not of my own volition. It did not identify itself, but was obviously James, who spoke most kindly of the work we both were doing to help promote an understanding of psychical phenomena. As in my London experience, I was listening quietly as I mouthed the words, remaining conscious but not instigating what was said.

As the message of commendation and inspiration continued, I began to feel embarrassed. After all, one didn't know just who or what was speaking, and if it was subconsciously originated then I was revealing myself to be an egotist and a braggart.

Finally this statement was made: "You are now ready to begin receiving a book by automatic writing, and if you will sit at your typewriter at nine o'clock tomorrow morning the communication will start."

When my own voice was returned to me, I promised to keep the date and did. Every day from then on for a week I sat at my typewriter most of the time, and in that one week the entire first draft of the James book was written through me. I had as witnesses to this fact the neighbors who eagerly gathered evenings to hear me read the new material that arrived each day. I take a week or sometimes longer to write one chapter on my own, so the speed with which this came seemed extraordinary. Although it was extremely tiring to allow James to use my mind for such long hours of work, what was coming through me was exciting enough to be worth any effort on my part to produce it. Yet when the entire manuscript had been written, I realized there was a great deal more effort ahead, since it wasn't in any great editorial shape.

"I hope you don't mind," I said to James at the end of the week, "but it seems to me we should go back and make some revisions."

"I hope *you* don't mind," James said to me, "but we are going to write a whole new book." So the same procedure was repeated in the following weeks—although this time he went considerably more slowly.

His newer effort dealt with the identical material, but it was now better organized, as if the original had been gone over and carefully edited and rearranged. Apparently he had found it easier in the first place to allow the words to flow through me when I was in an especially receptive state, even though everything had not been received entirely as he wanted it. From then on we continued off and on for a long time to edit it even more scrupulously. He would work a week or two and then let me rest for several weeks or even months, and then resume. Thus I came back to it each time refreshed.

The way our editing is always done is interesting, and to me somehow evidential in itself. As we are writing, the typewriter may stop in the midst of a sentence. I will wait for a few seconds, wondering what is wrong. Then I'll say, "Did we make an error?" In my mind a "yes" may be heard at this point, and so I will move the typewriter carriage back to the beginning of the sentence. Then I use the space bar and move along word by word until the typewriter stops again. I cross out that word and let him write in his correction, then we go ahead with the forward flow.

Of course, I would never presume to change James's text without his permission. If anything is not clear to me or is too wordy, or difficult to understand, I tell him and he rewords it. Unless, as he sometimes does, he remains adamant that he has written it exactly as he wants it. Often he is willing to accept my suggestion that he should more fully elucidate some obscure point. Sometimes I have asked questions raised in my mind by his statements and he has given a good bit of new data in order to clarify things for me.

Some people think that any entity attempting to communicate from the spirit world is omniscient and thus all his sacred words must be left intact. However, even the very best mediums may color the material unwittingly, and anyone who receives should be wary of this at all times. James indicates by his way of writing just how human he is, and this is actually part of his aim. He wants us to be aware that he is still a man, but now a man invisible, who has a certain amount of information to impart about little-known and little-understood aspects of the universe.

Some have wondered why, if he is the spirit of a man who died in 1910, he can now talk intelligibly about television, radio, jet airplanes and such. It is because his interests have been close to Earth interests and he has seen from his special vantage point everything that is going on here. This merely confirms his statements about how close he and his companions are to our plane of existence.

Some critics have complained that none of the writing using his name sounds the way the Harvard professor himself wrote when here. Why should it? In the first place, he's had innumerable new experiences. He has now progressed, he says, "as have all those who were his intellectual idols, to where they all know a great deal more than they used to when they were writing their happy little hearts out on Earth."

Sometimes James gets a bit frisky and a sentence like the above comes across more like my writing style than his, but he declares they are his own words. However, as I've noted, a medium almost invariably unconsciously "colors" what is filtered through his or her mind, so actually it's my fault that James's personal writing style is not evident as he runs his data through me. Those who don't know the intricacies of channeling don't understand the difficulties of getting immortal thoughts through mortal minds. A medium has to be in almost a deep trance in order for messages sent through him or her to arrive in pristine condition. And I am not even a true medium, just somebody able to service a couple of spirits. It is as a former newspaper reporter that I've been of value to James, because he wants to provide a clear-cut, straightforward account not prettied up with fancy prose. Obtuse phrases don't come naturally to me, which is just as well. Many people think that if the writing from alleged spirits is incomprehensible, it must be wise, but the language James uses with me is always simple and direct, and, I'm confident, all the more profound because of it.

But why was I, Susy Smith, the one to receive this information? Mostly because I would be willing to work the long hours and years required to produce it, but also (and this is the most backhanded compliment I ever received) because, my communicant implies, I was so dumb. James says it helped that I had given up on religion and philosophy and had read almost nothing on those subjects since my college days, so my mind was like an empty sieve through which he could strain his thoughts onto the paper in front of me. I am told that one of the big problems of most spirit communication is that it has to fight the preconceived opinions of the recipient.

Early in 1956, my first year of attempted typewriter communication, my hands used to be picked up from the keys before we started to write and held for a moment in the praying position. At that time I definitely did not believe there was a chance that there was any kind of a God who might be paying personal attention to me if I approached him through prayer, so the significance that sign was supposed to have escaped me. I finally decided it was probably an identifying signature of the communicant.

Now when I sat down to start receiving the material for James's book, my hands were first lifted from the typewriter keys in the same praying position, and at last I understood it. During the years since, my indoctrination in the wisdom of approaching God for loving assistance had been completed, and I knew that prayer was also the best way to protect myself from any unenlightened entities who might try to intrude their thoughts upon me. So I was willing to cooperate, and thanked James for reminding me to clear the air before making any effort to communicate. I immediately started a regular habit of asking Divine Consciousness for help before each typing session and then stating firmly aloud that nothing could come near me or in any way influence me that did not come from God in love and peace.

I also insisted that contact could only come with wise communicants who would give me the truth. My sincere desire to transmit only *facts* about conditions after death has been very strong as the writing flowed through me.

The material I am referring to here was eventually published as *The Book of James*.

James's main premise was the importance of continual personal striving for self-improvement, on Earth and in the spirit world. He wrote:

> For much too long your psychiatrists and behaviorists have attempted to convince you that man is a mere machine, or even an animal. It has been forbidden by your intellectuals to discuss man as a soul or spirit living in a physical body. One has been looked on as naive if he believed in a life after death, in a soul that could continue to live forever.
>
> It has been evident in recent years that this idea of man as a mechanical unit has given little harmony to the world, no peace and much dissatisfaction to men, for a theory so nihilistic cannot bring happiness. Now you are beginning to realize that in order to survive as individuals it is necessary to have a philosophy, to know that you are of importance in the scheme of things. There is no way that you can achieve true happiness and peace of mind until you once again return to the old concept of man as a spirit or consciousness which survives death into a Heaven of love and joy. When you become aware that the plan of the universe is a perfect plan and that you are a fundamental aspect of it, you will recognize your worth and that of all others.

James said that no soul is ever lost for all time, no matter how vicious or cruel he had been on Earth. Each must eventually, however long it takes, improve himself to the point of perfection. God will not allow any part of Himself to be thrown away permanently. He wants it all back.

> No one who knows that all men are designed to return to Ultimate Perfection can ever belittle himself or his fellow men. No one with such knowledge would

be able to use his authority to declare war, to kill, to in any way deliberately harm another, to do anything which will hinder the perfect growth of all other human beings and the world in which they live. When one thinks of himself as one with Supreme Intelligence he will act in a responsible manner at all times. In all things such men are peaceful, loving, kind, wise, and responsible. No such concerned man will make his own causes more urgent than those of another, nor his own needs more important. Your ecology problems will resolve themselves when each man thinks more of his neighbors and his neighbors' property than of his own. Your pollution situation will be remedied when care for all the world's beauties and bounties is more important than gain for any individual or group. Overpopulation will recede when all people learn not to have children until they are able to raise them properly under ideal conditions.

There will be no social injustices, no inhumanity to man, when all are known to be kindred consciousnesses with the identical beautiful destiny.

James was just like Mother in urging constant positive thinking. He felt that an acceptance of spirit survival and continued existence after death was going to make everyone on Earth think differently about himself and change his living habits—especially by learning positive thinking and practicing it.

Because I'm an arguer, it was natural for me to play devil's advocate for James, even while agreeing with him for the most part. But the more I've practiced positive thinking, the more I realize how difficult it is to do it all the time, and yet it does bring enough peace of mind that it is worth any amount of hard work.

James gave me a new point of view about all the illnesses suffered in my life, allowing me to endure them with more fortitude. He made me see that I probably wouldn't have accomplished as much writing if it had not been necessary for me to spend most of my time at home taking it easy on a couch or typewriter chair. Before having the strep infection, I was on my way to being a party person, for sure. I loved dancing more than anything, and horseback riding, tennis—good outdoor stuff like that. If I'd still had a healthy body when I got rid of my doofus husband, a life of activity would no doubt have been my goal, or another marriage and a family of children.

Fortunately, I've never lost that enjoyment of life, even though it has been endured mostly from a sitting position. My humorous outlook has been maintained in my books, even while writing a vast amount of serious information from James about the Hereafter. I don't know just how I could have hung on without humor. James has told me that one of the reasons he likes to work with me is that for both of us it is a pleasure rather than a chore, even though we have been discussing the deepest subjects. Though I live with pain, my mind still likes hanging around keeping in touch. But it can't be too long until my main activity will be trying to send that secret messenger from Heaven, or somewhere similar, so someone can win $10,000 by breaking my code.

I've done the best I could with this old body, which doesn't respond as it should to all the positive thinking I can muster. It hasn't even accepted the spiritual healing many have tried on me. Still I manage to keep going no matter what.

Bill Hanemann once wrote me to say, "The reason the study of psychical phenomena appeals to so many people is because it exalts the human ego, making a man feel that he's something beyond his ordinary crummy self."

"That's absolutely right," I responded, charged up with large doses of philosophy from the Other Side. "It does this because he is something beyond the ordinary crummy self he allows himself to be. If he would recognize that he is actually a spiritual being with a soul, he would live accordingly, and be exalted."

Bill's reply was a few complicated sentences that added up to a total comment of "Oh, yeah?" He was never one to be convinced without definite scientific evidence. So many people are like that, and my cherished hope is that science will some day support religion in the certainty that man survives death. Wouldn't it be a miracle if someone breaks my after-life codes? This idea doesn't seem as ludicrous as it might have years ago, when psychical phenomena were considered to be so far outside the scientific scheme of belief that they had to be categorically denied in order to protect the system. Yet even then, one of the country's most prominent philosophers, the late Professor C. J. Ducasse of Brown University, of whom I was very fond personally and for whom I had great admiration because of his wise and open interest in the psychic field, said, "If the facts do not fit our logic, it is time to reexamine our logic."

It was exciting to learn a few years later that the Parapsychology Association has finally been accepted for affiliation with the American Association for the Advancement of Science. So now the simple investigation of ESP—telepathy, clairvoyance, precognition—and also psychokinesis, is attaining a certain amount of scientific recognition.

But I wouldn't be surprised if the physicists arrive at the point of accepting survival research before the parapsychologists do.

A friend of a friend of mine had the unusual psychic experience of seeing her spirit father when she was at the point of death after an automobile accident, and she was suddenly and miraculously healed. Later she went to a Harvard professor of psychology for an explanation and his reply was, "I'm sorry I can't help you. Unfortunately, we're still working with white rats and dogs. We won't get to incidents like yours for a hundred years."

But that might be an unusually pessimistic statement for these times. With the mental climate of the world what it is now becoming, more and more people are looking for answers to life's questions, and a fantastic number are finding that psi opens the way to philosophical discoveries.

The kinds of things James discusses with me occur to a great many people. They don't necessarily happen only to those who are neurotic, uptight, ill-adjusted or under pressure. I hadn't been boozing or tripping on dope, wasn't living on happy pills or pot or sleeping tablets or speed, and only took LSD once, under fairly clinical conditions. I didn't even smoke cigarettes or dip snuff!

No, I had these experiences by deliberately inviting them, feeling myself to be making a systematic investigation of a new field of challenging interest. I knew from the first that it would be difficult to be impartially objective, because I wanted some rational scheme of life after death to be true even when not consciously admitting it to myself. That's why such a point was made to observe all events critically, to read more of the "con" than the "pro," to have frequent discussions with those who did not believe, and to argue with myself over each new manifestation.

As revealed by my efforts recounted in my books, such personal research takes a tremendous amount of patience, but it is fantastically rewarding. I don't claim that the incidents that occurred to me are necessarily convincing of spirit survival. Many of them, taken individually, would surely indicate coincidence and nothing more. Yet collectively there is such a large volume of curious happenings that coincidence hardly seems to be the answer. As Camille Flammarion, the famous French astronomer and psychical researcher, said: "When well observed incidents multiply, coincidence disappears."

One thing that can be said about these episodes is that they *have* been well-observed. If they didn't want to get themselves itemized, classified, labeled, and written down in books, then they shouldn't have started happening to someone trained for newspaper work who would make every effort to validate them.

It is only when you learn more about this subject personally that you are likely to accept it. Most people who look at it only superficially reject it completely—as I did before beginning my study. I had resisted for years the idea that those who die, if by chance they still continued to exist at all, might have any possible interest in Earth people and their affairs. I'd hoped they'd have something better to do.

Many who are somewhat interested but have not yet developed their psychic sensitivity to the point that they can communicate, or who, being warned of the possible dangers, do not wish to try it, have asked me how they can become conscious of the presence of their guardian angels. Nothing better can be offered than what Mother originally suggested: expansion of your awareness with a mental reaching out and surging, which will almost invariably be successful if you don't give up too soon. Most people do not have much patience for that sort of thing. If they don't get results immediately, they doubt that anyone who loves them is really there. I can only say, don't despair. Everyone who reaches out with warmth has someone there who comes in love and peace. But don't forget to wrap yourself in protection before you start your efforts.

After learning about the system from Mother and James, it is easy to understand the idea of gradual transition as part of an intelligent program after death—Evolutionary Soul Progression, they call it. A new definition for ESP. It was a wonderful concept with which to close our work. After we were satisfied with *The Book of James*, I sent it to New York and it was accepted and published by G. P. Putnam's Sons. It has been my most popular book, and over the years since, countless letters have come from readers whom it has helped. What a blessing James gave us all. Thank you for your hard work, my invisible friend.

It was about time to start doing something to try to prove all this interesting information that had come over the years. The seed for the codes had been planted, but it was hidden in my mind for a while. I had a lot of other things to do first.

THIRTY

THE SRF COMES INTO BEING

In 1969 I spent two weeks in Mexico City giving a few talks and radio appearances. When I lectured for the American Club, host Lee Nichols introduced me as "the Auntie Mame of psychical research." Although surprised at this glamorous and amusing designation, I told the audience it was gratefully accepted and that I would be delighted to live the role to the hilt, so if anyone knew any millionaires—any *single* millionaires—please to bring them around and introduce us. They didn't, of course. Nobody ever has any of those to spare.

The following Sunday I was sitting with Lee and his wife Grace in front of a large open fireplace, relaxing and basking in the glow of the flames. Lee, who loved to tease, said, "Just look at you, sitting there being Auntie Mame."

My answer was, "I'm not anti-anything. I'm too blissful."

The fact is, Mexico so enchanted me that I sold everything except what would fit in and on top of my car, a secondhand 1962 Cadillac Coupe de Ville, and went back that August to live in Cuernavaca. It is a delightful town forty-five miles down the mountain from Mexico City. The appeal was the spectacular beauty of the country, the charm of the people, and the stimulating climate. I never felt better in my life than while I was there. So why did I leave? I wrote a book. An editor from Macmillan indicated that he wanted me to do one for him, and *Confessions of a Psychic* just happened to be in progress again at the time. Several months later it was ready for his viewing, so I packed my car and headed for New York City. Macmillan bought *Confessions* and it came out in 1971, and the nicest thing happened then. If it sounds like bragging, so be it. My friend Frank Bang attended Marble Collegiate Church on Fifth Avenue in New York and he gave a copy to its well known pastor, Dr. Norman Vincent Peale, the *Power of Positive Thinking* man. And Peale loved it! He wrote me a beautiful letter of appreciation, and in his letter to Frank he was even kinder. Here are just a few of his words referring to the facts that *Confessions* vividly described both the risks and the challenges of mediumship: "This courageous work proves her to be a sensitive person of a high order, gifted with profound qualities of insight and a master of intuitive truth."

After the contract was sold, and before *Confessions* was completely finished, I had to find some place to live. After Mexico's fabulous climate, New York's weather wouldn't do, so this time I chose California. San Diego seemed ideal for about six months. Then my back acquired a muscle spasm that wouldn't quit.

It may sound pretty far-fetched to have been chasing around the world trying to find a climate that wouldn't hurt me too badly, but why not? When you don't have a family to hang on to and can write books anywhere you find yourself, why not, I ask?

Then came Tucson. A woman wrote me saying she had heard me lecture in San Antonio for Theta Sigma Phi (the former name for Women in Communication). I had been asked to speak there on my way to Mexico the year before. She said she and her husband were living on a ranch just outside of Tucson and would like to have me come visit them. It isn't as surprising as you might think to have invitations to visit strangers when you travel around the country giving talks. Still, it sounded impractical at first. But as my back kept knifing in the coastal dampness, and memories from my college days of southern Arizona reminded me of dry warmth, the trip seemed more logical. Finally I flew over to visit the nice lady, and in two weeks my back was normal. I went right back to San Diego, packed my car and moved to Tucson.

Would you believe that in 1971, this city didn't have a single vacant apartment complex with a pool? Now it's overrun with them. Anyway, in order to find a nice location with a place for my daily swim, I bought a double mobile home, and it came with furniture they let me select for myself. Of course, I moved from there in about ten years, but I didn't leave Tucson. I won't leave Tucson until they shovel me out. I joined writers' clubs, played bridge, swam a lot, did a lot of oil painting and book writing and made several pleasant lecture tours to Hawaii and Alaska, among other places.

Even with all this going on, I still didn't feel comfortable not making an effort to prove survival, so in my desire to accomplish something worthwhile, I started an organization whose goal is to prove scientifically that there is life-after-death. It is true that finding proof is the most difficult thing in the world to do; still, somebody, someday, is going to achieve it.

So in 1973 I officially established a tax-exempt, nonprofit Arizona corporation called the Survival Research Foundation (SRF). The idea was discussed thoroughly with my friend Frank C. Tribbe, a U.S. government lawyer who knew how to take the proper steps and write the proper papers, and he helped me tremendously. As its first president, I asked a group of fellow researchers throughout the country to be on the board of trustees—an Army colonel, a minister, some lawyers and their wives—people all deeply interested in the subject.

The outside of the brochure we published said:

*If you knew for sure you would live after death,
would you live your life differently?*

*What would it take to convince you
that life is forever?*

*Do you think that scientific proof of life after
death would change the world for the better?*

*Wouldn't you like to help add to the rapidly
growing body of knowledge in this area?*

*The Survival Research Foundation is dedicated
to an attempt to prove life after death.*

Here were our stated goals:

1. To conduct, subsidize and assist in the procuring
   of scientific evidence for conscious survival of the
   human soul or spirit after death, and to establish
   the results of the research as worthy of public con-
   sideration.

2. To establish survival research projects involving scientists and professional researchers interested in
   areas of psychical investigation other than those
   already significantly explored by parapsychologists.

3. Dissemination of information about such accom-
   plishments of this Foundation and others in the
   most constructive and sophisticated manner,
   because misapprehensions about our field are widespread among the public and should be corrected.

We built up a good membership and got some interesting research going, primarily at first in taped voices. Our most

interesting project, however, was the devising of a code, the idea being that those who left us a secret message (also called a key phrase) sealed in an envelope to be put in our safe deposit vault would, after their demise, try to send it back through a psychic or medium. If the key phrase that revealed the message was received, it wouldn't actually *prove* their survival in Heaven, but it would be a mighty good indication of it. Two of our most brilliant trustees devised the coding system—Clarissa Mulders, a Phi Beta Kappa teacher from Los Angeles, and Frank Tribbe. A number of people have sent their codes in over the years, but Clarissa is the only one who has since died, and so far, no word has come from her as of this writing. That doesn't mean it won't ever happen, especially now that we are using a computer to take care of the whole process. There are vast numbers of people registering their secret messages with us. Surely codes will begin to be broken.

I sent out SRF newsletters regularly and did research with a local group who actually got some kind of faint, unaccountable voices on magnetic tape, but it was nothing that could be proved. Although you may find it difficult to believe, a good bit of very interesting work is currently being done by many in the United States and Europe in electronic spirit communication. Voices, letters and clear images are being received through computers and fax machines and telephones—even on television screens. There is a big future for this, but possibly not in my time.

THIRTY-ONE

READY TO GO

With my foundation and traveling and writing a couple more books, I didn't have contact with James and Mother for about five years except for occasional messages of love and greetings. Then in February 1976, on an impulse, I layed my hands lightly on the typewriter keys, and James was there. We wrote together for three months and he gave me some good material, which he assured me we'd use in another book someday. I just laughed, sure I'd run out of steam for any more of the strenuous effort that would take.

My correspondent was disappointed when our sessions were terminated, but early in June I had an appointment with an orthopedic surgeon to get a new hip. I waited until turning sixty-five, then took advantage of Medicare right away. Mother and James gave me pep talks on how to handle the operation effortlessly by thinking of myself as a child of God who is immortal (but not yet ready to try out the immortality bit). I was told to hold constant thoughts of the success of the surgery and was promised that they would hold them also. This must have worked, because even though it hurt a lot, it wasn't a particularly trying ordeal. Now I have a successful total hip replacement and legs of equal length! I still had to use a cane because of the nearly atrophied muscles in the left leg, but was walking more like folks again. Soon I was taking care of SRF business and doing my usual amount of writing and traveling for years afterward.

Then one day I looked in the mirror and realized that I was getting old. The strange thing I've discovered is that age is very elusive. Oh, my body knows I am older, in spades, but my mind still feels just as young as ever—even today, twenty years later. It's still a shock, though, to see this chubby white-haired woman looking back at me.

Mother told me when she was sixty that one doesn't feel any older with the years, that she stayed the same in her mind. I looked at her lined face, her graying hair, her gnarled fingers and knew that behind that aging facade was the same warm, lovable, wonderful woman she had always been. But a youngster? That was hard to believe. She was right, however. Our bodies might not claim the lively persons inside, and our activities have to be limited by what we're physically able to do, but the quality of our inner lives doesn't have to change at all.

It did seem sensible to slow down a bit, though, so I wisely gave up the job of running my foundation. Luckily the presidency of the SRF passed into the hands of Dr. Arthur Berger, a Miami lawyer who over the years has built it into a world-recognized, respected organization. Then, because it seemed that a lady of my advancing years should live where there were people around in case she fell or lost her marbles or something crucial like that, I sold my manufactured house and moved into the Cascades, a retirement home.

My final discovery there was that you can get awfully tired of old people in masses. They tend to talk all the time about their aches and pains, just as I seem to be doing here. I got a virus the week after Christmas. Col. Frank Adams, for whom I was editing a book on the Shroud of Turin, came by and found me so debilitated that he and his wife rushed me to the emergency room at El Dorado Hospital, where I spent a week on IVs because of this unknown virus and being completely out of potassium. I was in and out of the hospital sixty-two days the next year, coughing constantly. Microscopic exams revealed that I had hemophylis, a form of influenza that was epidemic during World War I. Without modern antibiotics, it had killed people by the millions. Now, I was told, only a thousand or so get it in a year. So where did I ever find it?

Neither of my guardian angels could communicate with me while I was in that ragged shape, and I was lonely for them. Feeling so sick and weak and coughing my lungs loose, why was I still hanging around? Believing my life's work was done, I truly felt ready to give up this physical frame and get on with the next realm of existence, and to me this wasn't a negative attitude at all. On the contrary, I was eager to start with my progression and see if my reception of all the things my guardian angels had told me had been accurate. I wasn't pushing it, you understand, but was ready nonetheless.

One day in July, shortly after returning from my last stay in the hospital, I was lying on the couch with the usual feeling of exhaustion, reading a gripping novel to take my mind off my discomfort. When a severe coughing attack came on, it was followed by a dark and dismal mood. There seemed no logical reason to still be hanging around here putting up with all this foolishness.

"Dear God," I started praying aloud, "please take me. Let me go over to those who love me. What good am I here? Please release me." The cough came again, a big gut-wrenching spasm. "Please Lord, let me die," I cried out, then added quickly, "but not until I finish reading this book."

Levity was just a way of showing grace under pressure, but the very next mail brought me a letter that made me realize my life wasn't entirely useless as long as it was involved with James. It came from a stranger, Bernardine (Bernie) Krieg of Irving, Texas. She started off by saying that it had taken her a little over five-and-a-half years to write her letter to me. She waited all that time, then by chance mailed it so it was received during my only period of depression in years. Can it be merely coincidence that she finally sent it just when it was needed most?

Bernie, who was fifty-one in 1976 at the time of her story, told me that she and her beloved friend Bill often visited Luchea's Occult Bookstore. One morning Bill had spent some time there roaming around among the books. Then he telephoned Bernie, suggesting they have lunch. She told him she would rather just drive around with him and talk, and this turned out to be a beautiful time of verbally reaffirming their deep feelings for each other. Within an hour, at 1:40 P.M. while they were enjoying their ride together, Bill had a sudden heart attack as he drove. Bernie had the presence of mind to pull the steering wheel toward the curb and turn off the ignition. Then she called the paramedics, but Bill was dead before they reached the hospital.

The next day Bernie was drawn back to the bookstore to see if she might somehow feel closer to Bill, who had passed so quickly out of her life. She was relieved to find the place empty of customers. "I sat for a few minutes and tried to achieve a contact with him. When I felt guided, I started to slowly walk around the room. When I had almost completed the tour, I heard Bill say, 'Stop!' I did, and quickly scanned the titles before me. Suddenly I found myself reaching for one—*The Book of James* by Susy Smith. The subtitle—*Conversations from Beyond*—seemed to be a significant message, so I turned the book over and read the information about the author on the back of the dust jacket. Above it was your picture. But, Susy, the real message came when I finished reading and somehow mentally received instructions to turn the book sideways."

Now who, when looking at the picture of an author and reading the blurb about her, would think to turn the book sideways, unless somehow inspired to do so? Bernie realized it was a message from her friend when she saw that the only thing to be observed when the book was held in that fashion was the fine print along the side of my picture, crediting the photographer "Billy Mitchell, Owensboro, Kentucky." Bernie wrote of her amazement, for "While my Love was not the man who took your picture, his name *was* Bill Mitchell, and I affectionately called him 'Billy' at times."

How could she not believe he had reached out to her to identify himself? It seems pretty likely that this man's spirit must have had a big hand in giving her the indication she needed that he still survived.

Bernie hoped I would publish this story bringing such wonderful survival evidence, and I promised to do it. Coming at the time of my deepest despondency, her letter convinced me there could still be some use for me in the world. "I'd better hang in there after all," I thought, deciding that my time to go would have to be put on hold for a while longer. I then listened to a friend who had been urging me to go to her chiropractor-naturopath. He put me on such massive doses of vitamins and minerals that I got cured within a month and was ready for whatever came next.

When my two-year lease was up, I moved from the Cascades to an apartment that had a bedroom with an alcove large enough for an office and a porch overlooking green grass and eucalyptus and pepper trees. And you thought desert country was all sand . . . .

With all my new invigoration I was ready for James when he popped up in 1989 with the idea that those notes that were hidden away somewhere could be used as a basis for a sequel to *The Book of James*. Oddly enough, my psychic abilities have improved to the point that I can now hear him talking in my mind just as I hear Mother. It seems that a period of rest away from work improves psychic abilities. Oh, yes, and it should be mentioned that the days of the intruding spooks were long gone, but I still always keep myself protected before contacting anyone.

For this new project I borrowed a computer and taught myself to use the word processor. The keyboard was so gentle it was a pleasure to my fingers, but the printer was asthmatic and only half operational and spent most of its time in the repair shop. So I was glad when I finally finished *Ghost*

Writers in the Sky and got rid of the temperamental apparatus. Then the book had to be sold and distributed and all that took time and maybe too much physical effort. My new artificial hip was about the only thing that wasn't complaining by then. My knees, after having spent so many years bearing all the weight for that old do-less hip, completely collapsed on me.

I can't remember exactly what James said as he thanked me for *Ghost Writers*, but I took it to mean that I'd finished what I was supposed to do on Earth and could soon join my family and friends in the Great Forever-and-Ever-Land in the Sky. Best news I'd had in years. I got the notion in my head so firmly that I began making plans—appointed an executor, wrote my will, and told my regular bridge-playing buddies that they would soon have to find a new fourth. I've been taking a lot of kidding since then, as I've continued to live on and on and feel so much better and have such interesting things happening in my life. Mother came through once again with the right thing to carry me during that painful period. I'm good about applying aphorisms and started repeating over and over this little statement that she told me to use: "The right thing will happen in the right way at the right time."

I'm not sure that even Mother expected what was going to explode next in response to it.

THIRTY-TWO

CODE ACTIVITY

I wrote Arthur Berger, the SRF president, warning him to be prepared for my imminent demise. He replied that my code experiment would have more authenticity if, instead of an award being offered only to someone who received my secret message after my death, an award was also offered for anyone who could break my code while I was still around. This should satisfy the theory that it had been procured telepathically from my mind before I died. So I put out a flyer offering $1,000 to anyone who could break my code by reading my mind now. After introducing the Survival Research Foundation and explaining the origin of my code, the flyer said:

> Many people have firm convictions about life in the Hereafter because of faith in their religions or philosophies. There are some, however, who find themselves unable to believe what can't be proved. And while the concept of ESP (extrasensory perception) is now widely understood, few individuals can conceive the possibility of messages coming from someone after death. Mankind has been trying for centuries to find a way to prove that purported communications from the spirit world are real. Usually some other explanation can be offered instead. In the case of the SRF ciphers, the likely response when a code appears to be broken

after death will be that someone had already read the message by telepathy from the deceased's mind before he died.

That's where Smith's offer comes in. She wants psychics to attempt to receive her key phrase now. Her message could be a line from a poem, a well known book title, a nursery rhyme or any other familiar quotation or saying. If her key phrase that will reveal her message is received and her code is broken while she is still alive, the winner gets $1,000. If no one is able to break the code and it is then broken after her demise, the Survival Research Foundation suggests that this will be persuasive evidence for her continued existence in the spirit world.

Mediums, psychics or anyone else who might have felt a mental rapport with me were given until October 1994 to receive the message, and many people tried, but none succeeded. I am glad, of course, that no one has broken the code since then, either. It will be evidence of my afterlife only if it doesn't happen until I pass on. But this flyer was the cause of a number of small miracles that have been happening in my life since. It is interesting to me that when the time is right for important changes, they occur, whether you are prepared for them or not.

The thing that began all this for me was that the *Arizona Daily Star* gave the flyer to one of their best writers. I had admired his classical music reviews in the paper for years and was glad when it was James Reel who phoned me. I am always reluctant to have reporters come to see me, because many who know nothing about the subject love to make the interviewee look like an idiot. One smartass from a weekly Miami paper blasted me by drawing out that I'm alone in the world, am divorced, and have been mildly crippled since I was 26. From that he produced a picture of a poor soul who had to reach through mediums and psychics for consolation from "the other side." He hadn't listened to a word I'd said.

But James Reel saw me as I was—a researcher with a scientific bent eager to make this code into a project of real value. He referred to it as "A great experiment!" The following Tuesday, January 3, 1995, the *Star* published his piece—a half-page article on the front of the *Accent* section. It was accompanied by a picture his photographer had taken—a few more wrinkles and curves than necessary. But I can't blame anyone but Father Time for that.

The article was seen by Dr. Richard Lane, an associate professor of psychiatry and psychology at the University of Arizona, who was familiar with some of the recent theoretical considerations of two of his fellow faculty members. He brought it to the attention of Dr. Gary Schwartz, saying, "This looks like someone you'd be interested in." Lucky for me, he was, and so was his wife, Dr. Linda Russek.

Gary and Linda called and took me out to dinner, and we found that we had many mutual ideas and interests. I thought for sure they'd phone soon again, but they didn't. They were head-over-heels busy, as I've learned is usual for them, teaching classes or coaching, writing papers for journals, and traveling out of town to meetings. Also, Linda's soulmate West Highland terrier died. So they had legitimate reasons not to get in touch with me. But I just put it down to one more rejection and went on clomping around the house with my painful legs, trying to keep my spirits up by reading mystery and detective novels and watching TV. I was just marking time until the prospective change in my condition to a Heavenly one would please hurry up and transpire. Then one day an electric scooter that had been on order for months arrived. What a relief! My home resounded with crashes and bangs as I bumped into furniture and squeezed through doorways learning to control it, but it took the weight off my knees and I soon began to feel almost like a human being again.

This new pep gave me the impetus to call Gary and Linda and put a message on their machine: "Did you guys die or something?" They responded quickly and began visiting me regularly, saying I needed someone to be on my side. Linda started making dinner for us on Sunday nights, and we got together fairly often after that.

The question soon arose: if we were going to be a family, how should the new member be known? Linda thought at first she might call me Auntie Mame, but that didn't seem to work. Then they tried "adopted grandmother" and I said I didn't feel grandmotherly, having never even been a mother. Sometime during this period of discussion I began coughing again with something uncomfortable in my chest. Gary and Linda had to leave for a weekend conference in San Francisco, but they gave me the phone number of their hotel and insisted they be called if I got worse and needed them.

The next morning my lungs were talking to me, making squeaky little sounds when I breathed and complaining bitterly when I moved. A nurse friend said on the phone she thought I should be in the hospital, and fifteen minutes later four paramedics arrived and took me away in an ambulance. You think when you reach a hospital someone is going to get to work on you, but all they did was tell me I had pneumonia, cover me with a blanket and sit me in a wheelchair in the lobby of the emergency room—for six hours! Then I was on a gurney in the ER for another five hours, until a bed was finally available at midnight.

During the wait, at 10 P.M., a nurse came and wheeled me to a telephone down the hall, saying some doctor was calling me from California. A cross Gary was storming at me, "I thought you were going to call us if you had trouble." I explained my predicament and he revealed that he'd phoned a friend and had him check hospitals to find me when I hadn't answered at home. Then Gary said firmly, "Linda will get the first flight out tomorrow morning and come and take care of you and don't you give me any argument." She did, too, and returned every day thereafter with chicken soup.

When the hospital released me, Linda took me home for a week and fed me vitamins, fresh fruit and vegetables, low fats and few sweets. She said she wanted me to last a while longer. I've tried to stay on that eating regime and behave myself foodwise, but I do need cookies now and then. Maybe more often than that.

As I got well, it was so warm and cuddly to have someone acting like family that I decided it would be nice to grandmother the both of them. They seemed to enjoy the arrangement, but admitting to it made me really face the fact that I'm an old lady, which is still a bit difficult for me to accept. We got a good laugh one day when Gary introduced me as his adopted grandmother to another oldster. She was hard of hearing and replied, "Your illegitimate grandmother?" We accepted that.

Gary and Linda also had me move across town so they wouldn't have to drive so far on Sundays, and they helped me find an apartment complex right alongside the Catalina Mountains

Then, still full of ideas, they announced, "Now that Susy has such a magnificent view, she ought to be inspired to write a book." They brought a computer they weren't using and showed me its intricacies. It was many times more complicated than the word processor I wrote my last book on, but it played a great game of solitaire. The story of my forty-four-year survival research wanted telling, and the codes had to be introduced. So here I was, doing my favorite thing once again.

During this time, in the Human Energy Systems Laboratory at the University of Arizona, The Susy Smith Project had been formed to pursue serious research on the possibility of human soul survival as a legitimate scientific field of inquiry. My part in all this was to prepare a Website that would give people the opportunity to register their codes on my computer. When my manuscript was finished, I was raring to go on that, but you don't dare rare with Gary. "All in good time," was his favorite expression.

To pass the days (it turned into years, actually) until this big project could be undertaken, Gary and Linda made me promise to write a novel that had been challenging my mind for years. I had never tried a novel before, but I've read enough of them to get a rough idea how to go about it. Talk about entertainment! I can recommend it as the world's best antidote to boredom. You can invent a bunch of characters and give them a setting and then just wait and see where they will take the story. I had heard novelists say that the characters take over, and they really do. In this case, I produced a group of people who crashed in an airplane and went into the Hereafter. I wanted to see what kinds of activities they might get involved in. Turned out they knew who set the bomb that blew up the plane and they felt the urgent need to get that information back to the authorities on Earth. How did they do that? It took a lot of interesting finagling on their part and invention on mine, but darn, that story hasn't found a publisher yet.

Just as the novel was finished, Gary's laboratory produced a delightful graduate student who knew enough about computers to teach me how to prepare the Website material for the Afterlife Codes, and I was off and running. Of course, we ordinary laypeople could not put the copy into operation. It took computer design services to do the technical work. They were not hired to do this until a year later.

In the meantime, The Susy Smith Project was being talked about here and there and caught the attention of two television networks. In February 1999, both A&E (Arts and Entertainment) and HBO (Home Box Office) sent crews to Tucson, particularly interested that science was taking a stand for survival research. For them the Human Energy Systems Laboratory tested five of today's best-known mediums: Rev. Anne Gehman, Suzane Northrup, Laurie Campbell, George Anderson and John Edward. HBO paid their expenses and they were taped at the laboratory giving readings under highly controlled conditions. Their results were statistically remarkable.

The HBO program, *Life Afterlife*, featured Gary's laboratory testing of the mediums and also Anderson and Edward holding sittings. I was glimpsed in a couple of unidentified sound bites. Interspersed were several professors giving pro and con opinions about survival research, and now and then there were shots of people aimlessly wandering about and looking strange. I presume this was the media's idea of the spirit world. Nothing was mentioned about The Susy Smith Project or the Afterlife Codes.

The A&E interviews were conducted by a gracious man named Lionel Friedberg, whom we all fell in love with, but it seems he is no longer with that network, and whatever he prepared involving us is still flopping about somewhere in the breeze.

Early October had become the focal point for activity when it was learned that the HBO program was to be aired then, so Hampton Roads rushed Gary and Linda's book into print with that publication date. A writer named Ann Japenga had done an article on the Afterlife Codes for the *USA Today* Sunday Magazine section, and it too was geared for October 1. Its purpose was to formally announce the start of actual registration on the Afterlife Codes World Wide Web, which had finally been technically prepared. Then, just three days before "pub date" of the article, Gary told me my whole project was not scientific enough and we would have to postpone registrations. "You'll think of some way to explain that it's not going to appear until maybe New Year's Day," he said. "We'll have a big splash then." And he left town the next day on a publicity tour.

Ann and I fiddled and fumed in telephone anguish and finally concluded that I should go ahead with a preregistration on the Website. It would save Ann's article from oblivion and might give me an idea of what kind of reception the actual registration would have later on. With a lot of rushing around, I got it done, and the response to the magazine article and the Website startled us with its immediate enthusiasm and support. In the first two weeks there were some 1,000 preregistrations, over 9,000 visitors to the Website, and over 200 e-mail letters, most from warm and caring people. We knew then the registration would be successful.

The preregistration home page had a line stating "Our Goal is Scientific Proof of Life after Death" and a link that said "Can science prove an afterlife? Would it interest you to be part of such a challenge?" Well, it turned out that the word "science" was an embarrassment. Gary got letters and comments from a few of his academic colleagues saying that there was no way to keep fraud out of the experiment, so it couldn't claim to be scientific. Knowing that, we had tried to apply controlled conditions to every aspect of it. What more could we do? As a scientist naturally would be at the suspicion that he was involved in something criticized as unscientific, Gary was very disturbed. He and Linda were already stressed out, and they had been during the whole process of writing their book, *The Living Energy Universe*, which was attempting the difficult process of addressing certain spiritual concepts from a scientific point of view. Now he shut down our burgeoning project until we could figure out some way to protect it from those who would reveal their secret messages before they died, or who would try in some other way to break the codes illegally.

Our friend Dr. Don Watson e-mailed Gary, "I don't see how we can make this into a traditional scientific experiment because we don't know what variables are involved, much less how to control them." I, too, felt that we could hardly apply any more scientific principles and methods to a subject of this nature. Don thought we could bypass the problem of making it scientific by providing direct data to the registrants and their potential survivors without the risk of overinterpreting those data ourselves. With this as a clue to keeping things as foolproof as possible by letting the participants take their own responsibility, we are now resuming registration.

Gary suggested as a safeguard some kind of questionnaire that would reveal the character, honesty and integrity of the person registering, and I got to work on that at once to write a bunch of questions that would interest those legitimately registering and bore those who weren't serious about it. I had no idea it would be such a delight to work on. Trying to prepare questions that would be adaptable to all varieties of people was interesting. What I've finally devised are one hundred questions; they are actually entertaining to go through and yet they're responsible and thought provoking. "It is a sincerity test for your heart," I say when introducing the questionnaire section of the Website. "It seems unlikely that anyone who isn't completely serious about it or just looking for the notoriety, would take the time to answer. And a person who would give his secret message away after enduring all this to register is a certifiable nutcake."

The home page of the new registration says AFTERLIFE CODES, The Susy Smith Project, Our Goal is Proof of Life after Death. Then it reads:

> In *The Nature of Life after Death* English author Allan Barham wrote: "I can conceive of no greater service to man than to provide him with a credible picture of a life beyond death; a life which reunites him with those whom he has loved and have died, which makes sense of his suffering and striving on earth, which points to love as the principle of the universe, and which shows a progression toward ultimate union with that love which is God."
>
> It was my thought that such a service could begin with codes that people might be able to send from the Afterlife to prove their continued existence.
>
> We'd love to have you register, but this is not a game or a contest. You won't win or earn any money from it. It is not a race for membership. There are no prizes. It is a service we are providing that will be of use to you only if you care enough for your friends and relatives to try to prove that you will still live after death. We are not offering anything here but the opportunity for you to leave a code that it might be possible for you to send back to Earth from the Beyond.

We used the Tribbe-Mulders Code designed in 1973 for the Survival Research Foundation. It involves a juggling of several alphabets and is extremely complicated to prepare by hand. I've done it and I know, but for today's computers it's just a breeze.

The procedure goes like this: first you decide on a brief secret message you would like to use (Tribbe and Mulders referred to it as a "key phrase"). It should be of enough significance to you that you will remember it after your death, and it should be fairly well-known to the public so that someone here could pick it out of the atmosphere or energy or whatever when you send it from there to here. An example of a key phrase you might use is "the power of positive thinking." It could be a line from a poem or a nursery rhyme or the title of a book, like *Life is Forever*. This is not your code, remember, it is your secret message that is the key to unlocking your code. When you have chosen it and are sure you won't forget it, and have definitely not told it to another living soul, you are ready to tackle the questionnaire. When you have finished that, you may register.

I hope readers of this book won't think that I'm going to try to register you right here and now. No, I'm saving that for your computer and our Website and hoping we will hear from you. www.afterlifecodes.com

In the registration process, the computer will combine your key phrase with the standard alphabet, and that combination is what it retains. It will then randomly choose a line from a book whose pages have been hidden within it for that purpose, and it will encode this line using the new alphabet. The result will be a jumble of letters that looks like gobbledygook, and *this* is your code. Nobody knows what it is or what it means except the computer, which has to be presented with the words of your original secret message to unscramble it.

Should a time every come in the future that you believe you have received the secret message from someone who has previously registered with us and then died, there is another form on our Website that you can fill out and the computer will check to see if it breaks that code. Should this wonderful event occur, researchers at the Human Energy Systems

Laboratory will welcome you warmly; but before any announcement is made of it, they will thoroughly investigate your background and that of the deceased sender, checking and double checking your honesty, infallibility, and integrity. This is the place where we make our pitch to the scientists to prove to them that we are not being taken in by fraud.

But if and when some proved responsible person does present a secret key phrase that unlocks the code of one of our deceased registrants, it hallelujah time! Then will come the cheers, drum rolls, whistles and fireworks!!

What I've been endeavoring to reveal in this book is my own lifetime effort to bring indications of the survival of consciousness to the place where they may be accepted as scientific evidence. If a code could possibly do this, even to some slight extent, it would be worth all my work and worry. Yet I suspect that the profound information Mother and James have given about life both here and there may be the most valuable thing in this book.

Archie Roy, a professor of astronomy at Glasgow University, says, "The greatest obstacle to acceptance of the reality of paranormal events is not lack of evidence but the belief, resulting from nineteenth-century science, that such events are impossible."

Still, who knows what wonderful secrets about the Hereafter this new century will reveal?

I am talking to both Mother and James these days whenever I ask for them. I usually have a brief chat with Mother most nights after going to bed and saying my prayers. (Yes, the agnostic Susy of years ago has a whole new attitude—a positive joy in everything I now know and believe about God.) Mother and I were recently discussing a title for this book, and I asked her opinion about using the word "Afterlife" instead of "Afterdeath"—sort of shying away from using the word "death" on the cover. Mother surprised me by saying, "Death isn't the dirty word to us that it is to you." Of course, that would be right, but I hadn't ever thought of it before from her present point of view.

As this work was being concluded, it occurred to me to ask Mother and James to give some encouragement to those who will be facing new concepts in this book.

Mother wrote:

> I want to tell everyone that coming to Heaven is the best thing that will ever happen to them, so look forward to it—but never so much as to take one's own life to get here. My daughter and I have been through a long and (for her) grueling experience trying to provide evidence for life after death. If the codes can top off our work with a real snapper, it will provide success for our endeavors. Everyone would benefit.
>
> I love my girl and I'm proud of her. Betty Smith

To ask James to say a *few* words is a good joke between us. He doesn't mind my teasing him, though. His sense of humor was famous when he was on Earth and it's still going strong. Here's what he said, and to me it's quite encouraging:

> This is your friend William James and I wish to congratulate you on the wonderful work you have done and will do in the future when you come over here. I have no doubt that someone will receive the key phrase that will break one of your codes or those of others who leave their codes with The Susy Smith Project. Those on Earth attempting to receive a secret message from the other side should sit in meditation every day. Who knows who might just get lucky. I will do everything I can to help all of you send your key phrases through when the time comes that you are here transmitting. We are already planning for mass cooperation. The words will be widely distributed here, and the thought power of many spirits will be centered on them. When one group stops

concentrating on them, another will take over. This will be a major production circulating from spirits in all parts of the world in many languages. It may be difficult for you to understand the potential here. There are thousands available to help you people. Don't overlook our usefulness. We who continue to exist in this first plane after death want to be of help to those on Earth. And we will help. Keep your thoughts on a successful endeavor assisted by many spirits and we will be there for you. Don't underestimate us. Positive thinking all the way.

It is nice to contemplate the idea that people on both sides of the veil, those living on Earth and those who have passed on, will be making an effort to collaborate with all of us who are preparing and leaving these Afterlife Codes. At this point in my life, after all my years of research with my spirit friends, I am comfortable with their declarations of participation with us and do not find it difficult to accept them as reality.

Having one code or several codes broken by messages that seem to give evidence that they come from the spirit world could change the way people think and live on Earth. We cannot claim that this will prove the survival of the human soul after death, but it will certainly do more to indicate it than has so far been achieved. Many who have lost their loved ones and are grieving will be overjoyed to have a real indication that they will be reunited when they pass over. Those who are afraid of the looming nearness of death will no longer be panicked if they know there is a real likelihood that they will continue on in some other phase of existence. Certainly those who have felt their time on Earth wasted if they have not achieved the spiritual development they tried to attain will be encouraged to know what James has told us about the evolutionary progression of the human soul.

The possibility of something even close to scientific evidence that will help the bereaved feel confident that a spouse or a parent or a beloved child is not lost to them forever makes my heart smile.

Research from Beyond: The Ultimate Challenge

By Gary E. R. Schwartz, Ph.D.
and Linda G. S. Russek, Ph.D.

Now that you have met Susy Smith, you can appreciate her vision—to be able to prove experimentally that we can connect and communicate with our loved ones who have departed and continue our relationships with them. When we first met Susy, we were intrigued by her personality and enthusiasm, and soon we were inspired by her ultimate challenge. Her many years of effort, with the presumed assistance of her deceased mother and William James, have led to preparing a computer program whereby anyone who wishes may leave codes that might possibly be able to prove the survival of the human soul after death. It interests us that her communicants suggest there will be active participation of many in the spirit world who will offer continued collaboration in these projects.

As we write these words, Susy is still bright and lively, with the goal to remain here at least a while longer. But she knows it won't be too many years before she gets the chance to learn whether all her research has been as fruitful as she now hopes.

In the meantime, when she asked us to write the introduction and conclusion to this book as her eighty-sixth birthday present, we agreed, but only if, as gifts for our respective birthdays over the next year, she would give us one more book—her thirty-first. She has since said "Happy Birthday" to us with her first novel. Titled *Crashing Into Heaven*, it is an engaging account of the problems a few newly deceased spirits have when they discover a pressing need to communicate certain information back to Earth.

If Susy's longtime research is to be ultimately successful, some sort of Afterlife must exist, and perhaps the successful breaking of her codes will indicate this. It humbles us when we come to appreciate that this woman has devoted most of her adult life to getting ready for the Afterlife–preparing for when she joins her regular communicants and their many departed friends to send proof that she still exists. Thinking of Susy, her mother, William James and God knows who else getting together to send encoded messages back to Earth strains our imagination, to say the least.

If any research challenges the methods of science and the mind and heart of humankind, it is research that requires active collaboration with the Beyond. If we do not allow ourselves to entertain these questions and raise these hypotheses, we will never design the appropriate experiments and therefore may never discover the answers. We created The Susy Smith Project because we decided that Susy's ambitious plan needed to be taken seriously. She did not invent the idea of using Afterlife Codes to investigate life after death. What she has done is stand on the shoulders of giants, so to speak, and from this height, taken a further look, peering with open eyes at a universe most of us have only dreamt about.

However, if this challenge is to be met, we need the help of all who care about matters of the heart and soul and are willing to approach the hypothesis of love from above from the perspective of the scientific method. We hope that by reading this book you will have come to know and care about

Susy and her life's work, and that these feelings may help you to receive her secret phrases after she dies, if such a possibility really exists. Now that The Susy Smith Project computer is operating to encode the secret messages for the general public, we also hope that there may be others whose codes are broken after their passing.

The project, as we have worked with Susy to devise it, is straightforward conceptually and sophisticated scientifically. Using the Tribbe-Mulders system, the computer asks you for your secret message, then combines its letters with the standard alphabet. It then takes a line from one of Susy's books and encodes it in that combined alphabet. The result is a confusion of unreadable letters, and that is your code. It can be understood only when someone provides your secret message, which, of course, you will not have revealed to a single living person before your demise. The integrity of this system is guaranteed by The Susy Smith Project at the University of Arizona. In addition, the amount of $10,000 has been deposited in The Susy Smith Project's name in the university's Arizona Fund by Robert Bigelow of the National Institute of Discovery Science. This amount, plus future contributions, will guarantee the continuation of the computer's code activity over the years. For the use of the computer to leave your code, there is, of course, no charge.

We are pleased that a true beacon of enlightenment, Dr. Elisabeth Kübler-Ross, the author of *On Death and Dying* and *The Wheel of Life*, has been among the first to send in a code.

All good experiments must have control conditions, and Susy's experiment is no exception. So, in addition to her secret key phrase, we have created two control phrases and enciphered them on the computer. One, which we will call a "control telepathy phrase" because we are tempting people to break it by reading our minds before we die, is known to Susy, Gary and Linda. After Susy passes over she plans to communicate her own secret message and not this control telepathy phrase. So if after Susy dies someone guesses the control telepathy phrase and not Susy's Afterlife message, we can infer that the phrase was picked up telepathically from the living (Gary and Linda) and not from the deceased (Susy).

The second control telepathy phrase is known only to us, not to Susy. If after Susy's demise someone guesses this control telepathy phrase, we can be quite sure it was picked up from the living (Gary and Linda). Of course, we have also encoded our own individual Afterlife messages and left them on the computer, to be broken only after we die.

Susy has called us her "forever friends," and needless to say, we hope she turns out to be right. Science and spirituality began as friends with the establishment of the Society for Psychical Research in London in 1882, but this interest has waxed and waned over the years. As we enter the new century, there is a strong movement to have science and the Afterlife become friends again.

The project described in this book is Susy's effort to bring the two together. We hope for humankind's sake that many of you will accept it and that leaving codes will become traditional so that many spirits will be attempting to send the messages that will indicate their continued existence. This is currently one of the best procedures we know of to attempt to prove the survival of the human soul.

How would we live our lives differently if we knew once and for all that "life is eternal and death is only a horizon," as Carly Simon's song suggests? In death, as in life, would we not wish to be united with those we loved deeply and lost? Can loving consciousness communicate from beyond the veil? What do you think after having read this book? Perhaps you, too, will plan to leave a code in hopes of alleviating the grief of those you leave behind.

About the Author

The author of 30 books, Susy Smith has been vitally interested inn ESP, parapsychology, and psychic research since the early 1950s. In her many popular books she has shared her enthusiasm with investigating-and communicating with-the spiritual worlds. A resident of Tucson, Arizona, and still active at age 90, Smith oversees the Survival Research Foundation, which she established in 1971 to procure scientific evidence for the survival of consciousness beyond physical death.

Index

Hampton Roads Publishing Company

. . . for the evolving human spirit

Hampton Roads Publishing Company
publishes books on a variety of subjects,
including metaphysics, health, integrative medicine,
visionary fiction, and other related topics.

For a copy of our latest catalog, call toll-free
(800) 766-8009, or send your name and address to:

Hampton Roads Publishing Company, Inc.
1125 Stoney Ridge Road
Charlottesville, VA 22902

e-mail: hrpc@hrpub.com
Website: www.hrpub.com